ATLANTA JOBS

featuring the

CAREER SEARCH SYSTEM . . .

Your source to Atlanta jobs!

Not another vague, indiscriminate list of companies, but a complete strategy on how to uncover and utilize every available source to your advantage:

-- Atlanta's primary hiring companies

-- Personnel agencies

-- Classified want ads

-- Government positions

-- Professional and trade associations

-- Network and support groups

-- Free job assistance agencies

-- Helpful publications

And more!

-- Resume, cover letter and salary history preparation, with examples of each

-- Interviewing strategies, including questions and answers

-- Company profiles, employment data and hiring procedures

ATLANTA

JOBS

featuring the

CAREER SEARCH SYSTEM

Stephen E. Hines

Career Publications
Atlanta, Georgia

Distributed by
LONGSTREET PRESS, INC.
2150 Newmarket Parkway
Suite 102
Marietta, Georgia 30067
404/980-1488

Published by Career Publications, P O Box 52291, Atlanta, GA 30355.

Manufactured in the United States of America.

Graphics and cover design by West Paces Publishing, Atlanta, GA.

All information herein is believed to be accurate and reliable. However, neither the author nor Career Publications assumes any responsibility thereof. Correction requests should be mailed to Career Publications.

ISBN: 0-929255-02-X

YOUR INPUT IS VALUED,

AND WE WANT TO HEAR FROM YOU!

ATLANTA JOBS will be invaluable to you now, and we want future editions to be even more helpful! Your comments, suggestions and experiences help make that possible.

We appreciate your previous replies, and most of those are included in this edition. If your comments or suggestions are incorporated in future editions, you will receive a complimentary copy.

Some topics to consider:

-- Which of the eight source groups described in the Career Search System were most helpful in finding your job?

-- Which ultimately secured your job?

-- Which personnel agencies were most helpful? Least helpful?

-- Are there any additional companies or industries you would like to see represented here?

-- Are there any professional/trade associations or network groups you know that offer job assistance, and that are not included here?

-- Any comments in general?

Mail your information to
        CAREER PUBLICATIONS
        P O Box 52291, Atlanta, GA 30355.

To be released in 1990:

THE CAREER SYSTEM GUIDE TO CHARLOTTE JOBS

JOBS -- JOBS -- JOBS:
THE CAREER SYSTEM GUIDE TO THE FASTEST-GROWING JOB MARKETS

For information or to order, write

CAREER PUBLICATIONS
P O Box 52291, Atlanta, GA 30355.

Also available:

Continuous updated supplements to *Atlanta Jobs,* Appendices C (List of Selected Companies) and E (Professional and Trade Associations), plus any new helpful information. This will include information on new companies moving to Atlanta. Send $3 to Career Publications at the address above.

TABLE OF CONTENTS

Chapters:

CHAPTER I

INTRODUCING THE
CAREER SEARCH SYSTEM

CHAPTER I

INTRODUCING THE CAREER SEARCH SYSTEM

Good news: Atlanta is a great place to live and has thousands of job vacancies!

Bad news: The word is out, and thousands of job seekers (latter-day carpet-baggers?) have descended on Atlanta.

Good news: There is a job in Atlanta for you!

That's not just hype. There are indeed innumerable career opportunities available in Atlanta, but the catch is how to find them. And that's not really a problem; it just takes knowledge, a plan of action and the commitment to see the plan through.

In the summer of 1970, I moved to Atlanta, ready to seek fame and fortune in the business world. I had been teaching high school social studies for the previous three years, and thus coddled in the world of academia, I had no concept of what was in the "real world." I did not know what jobs were out there, or what companies offered them, and least of all, I didn't have the slightest idea how, where or what to do to find my new career.

I wish I'd had a book like this!

In the years since that summer, I have worked in personnel recruiting and placement. I have seen thousand of applicants struggle and stumble, trying to advance their careers--expending too much time, energy and money, and going in pointless directions. Finding a job is just not that hard-- if you know what to do!

But of course, most people don't. They have limited knowledge and resources from which to draw. I am always surprised at how otherwise extremely capable executives often produce the worst resumes, and go on to interview poorly! Even corporate personnel administrators, whom one would expect to know what to do, appear to be just as much in the dark as everyone else.

The purpose of the **Career Search System** is to fill this vacuum of misinformation and lack of information, and to provide job seekers with knowledge needed to successfully conduct a job search. This System represents nearly twenty years of knowledge, gained almost entirely from that best teacher, experience. I have compiled the arcana, simplified and methodized it, and the result is the **Career Search System.**

What is the **Career Search System?** It is a step-by-step, hand-in-hand practical guide to finding employment. Whether your objective is finding a new career, advancing your present career, or rebounding from a lay-off, the **Career Search System** will guide you to the best job available.

Within these chapters, you will discover all the information needed to obtain the right job in Atlanta. Outlined in detail are the who's, what's, how's and when's, that will result in the job you want. Many sources are revealed that you probably never considered or knew existed. Even if you were aware of them, you may not have understood how to benefit from them.

The **Career Search System** will give you the tools you need to apply in your job search. You have only to use them, following the guidelines and directions.

There is one requirement: the firm commitment to find the job best suited for you. And that requirement will include work. You may hear many times, "Finding a job is a job in itself," and that is so true.

But since most of us would rather play than work, let's get into the spirit of job hunting with a little game, on pages 14 and 15.

Now back to the real world! I hope this exercise has shown you what is ahead in your job search. As this is a practical guide, I cannot help you in assessing your abilities or need and wants. Once you have finished that, my system definitely will get you the rest of the way!

The Career Search System

The Career Search System consists of four basic steps that will lead to job offers. Each step is discussed fully, describing in detail exactly what you should do.

Step #1 in your job search is to prepare your resume--not just a good resume, but a "better" resume: the "Power Resume." As you will read in the resume chapter, the first contact you make with a company is usually through your resume, and that first impression must be positive. Each section of the resume is discussed in detail, explaining how, when and why you use each, so that your resume will make the best first impression possible. Even if you plan to have a service prepare your resume, carefully read this chapter, so that you can give to the service the layout and standards you expect to be followed. Numerous examples are shown in Appendix A.

Step #2 is developing a marketing strategy to obtain interviews. If you have never been in sales and marketing before, you are now! Using a looseleaf notebook to record your efforts and results, you will begin to develop contacts and sources in order to obtain interviews. The System gives you far more sources from which to develop leads and interviews than you will probably use, but they are all there if you need them. Start with the ones that are the simplest and easiest for you, and if you are not satisfied with those results, use the others. The System even indicates which sources work best for different backgrounds, and so you can choose the one(s) best suited for you.

Once your marketing efforts are into full swing, you will begin to be invited for interviews. *Step #3* contains information on the preparation you must do before that interview, as well as the interview itself. Numerous questions, suggested answers and the reasoning behind the questions and answers are discussed fully. If the very thought of interviewing makes you break out in a cold sweat, then relax. The **Career Search System** will have you well-prepared, and will carry you through the interview with flying colors!

CAREER

**Start Here!
Move 1 space.**

ASSESS YOUR ABILITIES:
Objectively—Move 2 spaces.
Non-objectively—Move 1 space.

STAY HERE UNTIL YOU TRY ANOTHER SOURCE

MARKET RESUME:
Move 1 space for
each interviewing source you use.
(MAXIMUM—6 spaces)

MOVE BACK &
FORTH A
WHILE, THEN
MOVE 1
SPACE.

2

sources are better than
one, but use another
source, then move
1 space.

Getting the Idea?
Use another source
and keep moving.

DITTO!

DITTO!

**JOB OFFER
YOU WIN!**

Go to church and pray no one
else has a good interview, and
then does good follow-up!

14

SEARCH

GO BACK TO START. GET HELP AND TRY AGAIN.

ASSESS NEEDS & WANTS
Realistically—Move 2 spaces.
Unrealistically—Move 1 space.

STAY HERE UNTIL YOU COME TO YOUR SENSES!

PREPARE RESUME
Poor Resume—Move back 3 spaces.
Good Resume—Move 1 space.
Better Resume—Move 2 spaces.

CONGRATULATIONS!
You Got an Interview
Prepared for interview—move 1 space.
Unprepared for interview—move back 6 spaces.

PREPARATION
Research only—
Move 1 space.
Research & Rehearse—
Move 2 spaces.

CLOSE
but we're not playing horseshoes! Move back 1 space.

GOOD INTERVIEW!
FOLLOW-UP—Move 2 spaces.
NO FOLLOW-UP—Move 1 space.

15

If you have always thought that once you finished the interview, your work was over, then think again! *Step #4* covers the follow-up procedure you should do after the interview, to give you an extra push. The "thank-you" note is discussed, as well as additional research and sources you can employ.

In addition to the four basic steps outlined in Chapters II, III, IV and V, Chapter VI discusses job-related correspondence, and numerous examples are given in Appendix B. The formats for thank-you notes and cover letters are given here, including different types of cover letters, each used for a specific purpose. When and how to include your salary information is also discussed.

Using ATLANTA JOBS

Think of this book as a workbook, similar to the ones you used in school. You should underline or highlight passages, write in the margins, fold down the edges of pages you want to refer to later--anything that will help you derive the most from the information contained here. In fact, by the end of your job search, this book should be thoroughly worn out!

Every job needs supplies, and this one is no exception. In addition to the basics, you will need the following:

-- loose-leaf notebook

-- highlighter-type marking pen

-- lots of paper

-- red marking pen

-- transparent tape

-- typewriter or word processor

-- telephone answering machine, so you will not miss any calls for information or interviews.

Conclusion

In the nearly twenty years that I have been in personnel placement in Atlanta, I have dealt with thousands of companies and their personnel representatives, interviewed thousands of applicants and read tens of thousands of resumes. I stress my experience so you will understand that I know what is going on, in your mind and in the minds of companies, and to assure you that I know what I am talking about! I have encountered the problems you're facing many times, and I can help you find the solutions!

Step #1 in your job search is resume preparation. Let's get started!

CHAPTER II

STEP ONE:

THE "POWER RESUME"

CHAPTER II

Step One: Resume Preparation

It's not what you know, but how you present it! Let me explain.

I recently ran a small, classified ad in the local newspaper for a manu-facturing plant manager. In response to that one short ad, I received over 100 resumes; a larger ad would probably have elicited many more! Obvi-ously, I did not have time to interview all of these applicants, or even to call them all. Many of them had the right background and experience, so what criteria did I use in deciding which to interview first? I used the same test that every other recruiter uses: the quality of the resume.

And what happens to the applicants with the poor resumes? I don't know, since I never call them!

Thus, you see that a resume has both positive and negative potential, and we can draw two conclusions regarding the resume:

> 1) A resume can get you an interview, which may ultimately re-sult in a job.

> 2) But a resume also can prevent you from getting an interview, and thus you will never have the opportunity to show why you should be employed there.

The importance of a good resume cannot be overstressed. Even if you have exactly the right background the company is seeking; even if you can interview perfectly; and even if you would make an ideal employee for the company, you will never get in the door if the company's first impression of you is negative, based on a poorly prepared resume.

Wow! Did you ever think that one sheet of paper could have so much power over your life and career!

But not only does you resume need to be "good," it also needs to be "better," that is, better than your competition. Imagine reviewing 100 resumes for just one opening! In order to peruse that many resumes in a cost-effective time frame, I tend to scan through the pile, and pull out the ones that look most appealing. Since a positive impression of the applicant has already been established, these "better" resumes receive more attention and sooner. The others may never even get read!

This chapter will explain how to write a "better" resume and how to use its power to your advantage. In short, you will learn how to write the "Power Resume."

So what makes up a "Power Resume"? There are many factors involved, and we will cover them in detail. In addition, numerous examples are given in Appendix A. First, however, let's discuss what a resume is.

Simply stated, a resume is

"A short summary of your positive qualifications for employment."

Now let's analyze that definition.

Short: Most applicants need only a one-page resume, or two pages at the absolute most. And yet too many job-seekers feel that a short resume implies a lack of experience, and conversely, a long one suggests a well-qualified applicant. Nothing could be further from the truth. In fact, a lengthy resume suggests a verbose egoist, unable to discern the important from the irrelevant! OK, maybe that's a bit severe! Truthfully, many job-seekers are probably not aware of what should and should not be in a resume. Perhaps that is why you are reading this! Bear in mind that personnel departments receive many, many resumes, and I assure you that from my own experience and from discussions with corporate recruiters, long resumes are seldom read. On the contrary, concise resumes get the most attention.

While on this subject, here's a bit of crazy logic: I recently interviewed a manager with a three-page resume. When I asked him if he ever read the three-page resumes he received, he immediately said "No!" He then went on to tell me that nevertheless, he was certain other managers would read his!

Summary: This is a resume, not your autobiography, and it should sum up only information germane to your job search. It should not include irrelevant information, such as your appointment to the college homecoming court or being selected "Most Eligible Bachelor," and do not include a photograph.

Your: This is *your* resume, not anyone else's. Do not mention the names and background of your family, spouse and children, or the name of your supervisor. (Incidentally, I once had an applicant who was rejected for an interview because his resume referred to "my lovely wife Lorain and our two adorable children, Mark and Susie.")

Positive: "Accentuate the positive," as the old song goes. A resume should emphasize achievements, accomplishments, honors, awards, etc., and omit any negatives. You may even wish to include a brief summary section, highlighting your best assets. Use positive wording, creating an up-beat image of yourself. If you were ever fired from a job, a resume is definitely not the place to reveal it!

Qualifications: Education, experience, personal data, references.

Employment: The finish line!

Preparation

Now that you understand what a resume is and what it can do, you can begin to assemble yours, by obtaining the necessary subjective and objective data. Objective data is listed below, but depending on your experience and job objective, you may not use all of it. In particular, the information on your college education will become less important as you gain more career-related work experience. Employment that occurred over ten years ago should be only very briefly included, in favor of your more recent experience, which should be discussed more fully. In general, this is what you need to compile:

    1) Address and phone number (permanent and temporary, if applicable)

    2) College information, including

        - graduation dates (month and year)

- grade point average (major and overall) and/or class ranking

- honors, achievements, elective offices, etc.

- percent of college expenses earned

- activities, including sports, clubs and professional organizations

- recent grads should list career-related courses taken or scheduled

3) Career-related seminars, courses and special training

4) Professional distinctions, honors, achievements, awards

5) Hobbies and interests

6) Activities, including membership in professional organizations and civic associations

7) Employment data, including

- brief description of your company(s) and its products/services, if not generally known to the public

- title or functional title

- dates of employment

- duties, responsibilities and descriptions

- accomplishments, awards, sales quotas, distinctions, etc.

8) Career-related experience, other than through direct employment.

Now is the time to plan whom you will use for references, and confirm with them. Three references are sufficient, probably one professional, one personal and one academic (for recent grads) or former employer.

In addition to that objective data, you need to assess you qualifications, strengths and weaknesses. Be honest with yourself and answer the following:

- Why should XYZ Corporation interview (and maybe hire) me?

- What do I have that other applicants may not?

- What do I do best? Worst?

- What are my best developed skills (judgment, communications, work relationships, decision-making, etc.)?

- What are the most important achievements and accomplishments of my life and career?

These answers are important in understanding your employment assets. Start planning how you might incorporate them into your resume.

Format

There is no one universal format used by all job-seekers, but rather basic sections that can be worded and assembled to fit each person's background. The information I have outlined here is very general in nature, and will result in a functional/chronological resume, the type most commonly accepted. However, under certain circumstances, you may wish to use a topical format, which will be discussed later. Most importantly, as you write your descriptions, keep in mind why you are writing this resume: to impress a potential employer and gain an interview. Thus, you want to include not only your basic qualifications, but also distinctions and achievements that put you ahead of your peers.

Name and address: At the top of your resume, center your name, address and phone number. Type your name in all capitals and use boldface in larger-size type, if available. Professional certifications, such as C.P.A., should be included on the line with your name (JOHN A. DOE, C.P.A.). If you have a temporary address (*e.g.,* a student) you can use that address and include a permanent address at the bottom or elsewhere, noting when it will be effective. If you are moving soon, you can use either your old or new address and phone number; just be certain that you always can be contacted by prospective employers. Needless to say, update your resume with the new address as soon as possible. If you feel comfortable receiving phone calls at work, you may include both your home and work phone numbers.

Objective: If you include an Objective, this will be the first section, after your name and address. If you are applying for a specific opening or in a specific industry, tailor your objective to fit. Remember, however, that if your resume states a specific objective (*e.g.,* sales) and you are applying for another (*e.g.*, management), you likely will not be considered. Thus, if you are not so sure about a specific objective, you can make it more open in nature. A better alternative used by many applicants is to prepare two or more resumes with different objectives, and use the one most appropriate. Or you can simply omit the objective all together, and open your resume with a Summary paragraph. In practice, I find that I tend to omit the Objective more and more often, in favor of a very personalized cover letter, and that is what I suggest you do also.

Summary: The purpose of a Summary section is twofold:

1) Summarize your abilities

2) Highlight your qualifications that propel you over other applicants.

A summary paragraph is optional, but it can be very effective, especially if you have some short, important data you wish the reader to see first, as an enticement to read further. Do not defeat its purpose by making it too long and thus lose its impact.

The Summary can be used with or without an Objective, or you can incorporate the Objective within this section. It should be very positive and up-beat, with an emphasis on abilities and achievements. Here are three examples, and more are included in the sample resumes in Appendix A:

Proven success in solution-oriented Sales and active Sales Management. Consistently promoted or recruited as a result of outstanding sales performance. Assembled highly effective and cohesive sales teams.

Recent college graduate in Business Administration with proven record of initiative and accomplishment. Completely financed all education costs through full-time employment, thus gaining five years of business experience. Seeking Management Development Program utilizing practical experience and academics.

Accounting/Finance graduate with more than four years accounting and auditing experience. Thorough knowledge of federal tax policies and procedures. Experienced with both manual and automated invoice systems, using Lotus 1-2-3 software. Seeking position as either Staff Accountant or Accounting Department Manager.

Education: You can use either Education or Employment as your next section, depending on which is the stronger or more important. For example, recent grads with limited or no relevant experience will place the Education section first. However, if you were a co-op student or intern, or have some other good business experience, list that first and Education next. More experienced applicants will generally place the Employment section ahead. An exception to this is that experienced applicants with a degree from a highly regarded institution could list Education first. As you gain more experience, the Education section will continue to shrink, as the Employment section grows.

For the recent college graduate with limited career-related experience, academics will be paramount, and thus will incorporate a large part of the resume. State the name of your college, the type of degree you will be receiving, major and minor concentrations, and month and year you expect to graduate. If you had a high Grade Point Average (above 3.0 on a 4.0 scale) and/or graduated in the top one-half of your class, include that information. Then list a few relevant courses that you have taken or plan to take. Earning a large part of your tuition and expenses shows initiative and should be mentioned. Definitely include honors, activities and elected positions. If you have more than one degree to include, list the most recent first.

Applicants with relevant work experience will list most of the same information, eliminating less important data with each new job and subsequent resume. Course titles will be the first to be eliminated, followed by activities and minor honors. For about ten years, continue to include a good Grade Point Average, important honors and elected positions. By then, your recent achievements will be more indicative of your abilities. If you are not a college graduate, I suggest you omit the Education section entirely, although you can include a reference to your academics in the Personal section, such as "Attended ABC University for three years, majoring in Business Administration."

After you have listed your academic institutions, then include relevant seminars and courses taken, and the dates. Also, include any professional certifications (C.P.A. , Professional Engineer, etc.) or awards gained through additional studies, and the dates bestowed. However, do not include certifications from previous careers that are not germane to your current job search; for example, omit references to real estate courses, if you are no longer pursuing that career.

Employment: Note: You may call this section "Experience" if you wish, especially if you are including experience gained through non-employment (*e.g.*, volunteer work), temporary assignments or part-time jobs.

All potential employers want to see some work experience, even for recent grads, and the more successful and relevant it is to your job objective, the better your chances of securing employment. List your job title, company name, dates of employment and description of job duties. That seems simple enough, but since it is the most important part of your resume, it must be perfect. Follow these guidelines, and refer to Appendix A for examples:

1) Use reverse chronology (last job first).

2) Be concise, and thus hold your resume to one page, if possible, and never more than two.

3) Don't get bogged down in details and don't feel you must include everything you have done. Save something for the interview!

4) Titles can sometimes be misleading; use functional, descriptive titles when necessary. For example, I recently prepared a resume for an individual who was managing the company's entire personnel function, although his title was only Personnel Administrator; I used Personnel Director as his title, to emphasize the scope of his responsibilities.

5) Be certain to include management and supervisory responsibilities.

6) Emphasize accomplishments, awards and achievements. Underline and/or use boldface on the most important.

7) List your last or current job date as "present," even if you are no longer with the company, unless many months have passed since your departure.

8) The most recent experience generally should have the longest description; experience more than ten years ago can be combined for brevity.

9) Percentages are usually more easily understood than exact figures, since the relevance of large and small amounts varies from industry to industry. Unless you are certain your readers will un-

derstand and/or be impressed with your figures, consider using percentages instead.

10) Do not list your reasons for leaving an employer, unless it makes a very positive point or explains several recent job changes.

11) Do not use acronyms or arcana that may be unfamiliar to most readers.

12) Include a brief description of your company(s) and its products/services, if most readers might not be familiar with it.

13) Numbers less than 10 should be written out.

14) Do not state your salary on the resume. However, some classified ads may request your current salary or a salary history, which can be included in your cover letter or on a separate page. (See Chapter VI: Correspondence.)

15) Since many companies shy away from individuals who have been self-employed, I suggest you avoid direct references to that. For example, you could describe your job title as "General Manager," rather than "Owner."

16) Use mostly "non-sentences" without a pronoun subject, and avoid using personal pronouns. Definitely do not write in the third person and avoid using the passive voice.

Personal: Although this section is optional, I suggest it be included if the information is positive and helpful. However, you can exclude some of your personal information, if you think that might be expedient. Otherwise, include birth date (not age, since that may change during your job search), marital status, height/weight and if you are available for travel. Unless there are absolutely, positively no circumstances under which you will consider relocation, I urge you to add that you are open for relocation; the reasons for including this are explained in Chapter IV: Interviewing Tips.

Do not mention potential negatives (*e.g.*, obesity) or restrictions (*e.g.*, geographic). Some states restrict including age, and you may omit that if you feel it could be a handicap, and the same is true for marital status. Never state your race or religion, but do include citizenship status, if you sense it may be in question.

Next mention a few hobbies and interests (reading, sports, music, etc.), that you are actively pursuing and that can be used to "break the ice" during an interview. (Then be ready to discuss them; for example, if you list reading as an interest, be prepared for the question, "What have you read lately?") If you are multilingual, add that here; if you are not quite fluent, you can describe yourself as "proficient." If you have several years of college, but did not graduate, you may mention that here. If you have excellent career experience and have decided to stress that in lieu of a separate Education section, you should list your college degree here. Finally, include memberships in professional associations and your civic involvements; however, do not include more than three, lest your priorities be called into question.

References End your resume with "References available on request." Do not list your references on the resume. If you get to the bottom of your resume and will have to crowd to add this final sentence, simply omit it or include it as the last sentence in your Personal section.

Topical Format

As I stated earlier, the functional/chronological resume is the most widely used and accepted form because it is simple and easy to understand. Under certain circumstances, however, the topical format may be better suited for your use.

The topical format differs from the functional/chronological format in that it includes an Experience section, either in addition to or in lieu of the Employment section. It can be especially helpful when you are changing careers or re-entering the job market, and want to emphasize skills you have gained that are relevant to your job objective. It also can be used to summarize what might otherwise be a very lengthy resume by combining many jobs into skill categories. And finally, it can be used simply to emphasize certain points or skills you feel important. Several examples of this format are shown in Appendix A.

I have recently begun to use more often a variation of this format, combining it with the functional/chronological. When doing so, I generally choose the two or three skills that best summarize my applicant's experiences or abilities, and include them under the heading "Qualifications." For example, I did a Communications Specialist's resume by summarizing her experiences in Marketing, Public Relations and Copywriting, and then listing her employment and a very brief description of the responsibilities of each position.

Synopsis/Amplification Format

This resume version consists of a synopsis page that includes all the basic information and sections, but with no details. The details of employment and experience are placed on a separate page, called an "Amplification." I receive these occasionally, and they are acceptable. I really don't recommend them, however, because invariably they get too long and so bogged down in detail that they are difficult to read, not to mention boring. As I have stated before, save the details for an interview, when you have the opportunity to personally explain your experiences.

Conclusion

In Appendix A, I have included many examples of excellent resumes, and I have tried to illustrate as many diverse situations and backgrounds as possible. But because each person's background is unique, do not try to copy too closely any example given. There are many acceptable variations of the basic format, and if you keep in mind your purpose in constructing a resume, you can vary the format to fit your needs.

In typing your resume, use a good electric or electronic typewriter, preferably a word processor with a laser or letter-quality printer and with proportional spacing. Do not use a dot-matrix printer. After you have finished typing, carefully proofread for errors and misspellings. Ask two or three friends to read it also, for suggestions and further proofreading. When you are satisfied, have the copies made at a local quick-print shop; it's probably cheaper than you think. Use a good quality of cream, light beige or buff-colored paper for best results, although plain white is certainly acceptable. Do not use parchment paper. Buy extra blank pages to use for cover letters, and envelopes that match your resume. Do not use green, pink or any other brightly colored paper. Above all, be certain the resume is neat and clean; remember, it represents you.

And finally, here are a few common mistakes I have observed over the years:

1) Without question, the most frequently misspelled word on resumes is liaison, probably misspelled on a third of the resumes I receive! The most commonly misspelled (and overused!) abbreviation is etc. (not ect.).

2) Another word often misspelled and misused is Bachelor. It does not contain a "t" (batchelor), and the degree is a Bachelor of Whatever or a Bachelor's degree, not a Bachelor's of Whatever. The same is true of Master's degrees.

3) The most common grammatical errors I observe are in the misuse of periods, commas, semicolons and colons, and the mis-

3) The most common grammatical errors I observe are in the misuse of periods, commas, semicolons and colons, and the misplacement of quotation marks. Unless you are positive you have used them correctly, I advise you to check with a grammar reference book. Three primary examples are these:

- Commas and periods are always placed *inside* quotation marks, and the reverse is true for colons and semicolons. The placement of question marks and exclamation points varies, depending on the usage. (Now that you know this, notice how often it is done incorrectly!)

- The word "however" is preceded by a <u>semicolon</u>, not a comma, when used as a conjunctive adverb, separating clauses of a compound sentence; however, a comma is correct when using "however" as a simple conjunction or adverb. If this sounds confusing--and it does to me!-- just notice how I have correctly used "however" throughout this book.

- Colons should be used at the end of a complete sentence, not a phrase.

4) Another frequent mistake is inconsistency in verb tense or parallel structure.

5) This is a resume, not a sales brochure. Do not use any format that looks "gimmicky." Use standard size 8 1/2" x 11" paper and do not write on the back of your pages.

If you still have questions regarding correct word usage, spelling or grammar, you can call Georgia State University's Grammar Hot Line at (404) 651-2906. This free service is staffed by professors who work the hot line on a volunteer basis between their regular schedule of classes. If your question cannot be immediately answered, the staffer will research the information and call you back.

Now let's go back to the question I posed earlier, "What makes up a 'Power Resume'?" The resumes in Appendix A are all good examples of "Power Resumes." Observe that they all follow these guidelines:

1) Proper layout

2) Concise, preferably one page and never more than two pages

3) Attention to detail, especially spelling, grammar and neatness

4) Emphasis on the positive (accomplishments, honors and achievements)

5) Relevance to the job objective.

The answer to the question is simple: Follow the outline and guidelines presented here, and you will have composed your own "Power Resume." My knowledge on the subject is first-hand, having read many thousands of resumes, written at least a thousand more, and consulted with other personnel recruiters to obtain their input as well. Thus, you can rest assured that your better and more powerful resume will get the best results possible!

P. S.

Now that you know what is involved in preparing your own resume, you may be concerned that it is too difficult and time-consuming for you, and you may be planning to have a professional resume service prepare it for you. Considering some of the home-made products I receive, I might encourage that also--but with definite reservations and qualifications.

In the past, I have been hesitant to recommend the use of resume services, because I have seen so many poor results. In fact, I recently discussed this with the former Director of Employment for a major Atlanta corporation, and who is now a training consultant. We were talking about resumes--specifically, the bad ones--and we agreed that some of the worst were "professionally" prepared!

Let me quickly add, however, that although I most remember those bad examples, I have also reviewed many excellent resumes that were prepared by resume services. A good, experienced resume service can be extremely helpful; just be careful with your choice. Insist on editorial approval and be certain it meets our standards before you accept it. Ask the background and experience of the person who will be preparing your resume, and request to see actual copies of recent work. Show them some of the samples I have included in Appendix A, to use as a pattern for your resume. The best of these services will have at least a word processor with proportional pitch and that can justify right and left margins. They also should have a letter-quality or laser printer. Better still are the ones using a personal computer that can do italics and variable-size type.

Although the layout and appearance are important, the paramount factor is the content of your resume. You can help in this preparation (and probably save money) by composing most of the content of your resume beforehand, and simply have the service do the re-typing and lay-out correctly.

Whatever you decide, remember that this resume represents *you*. If you have the time and feel competent, use the information I have outlined and make your own resume. It's really not as difficult as you might imagine. Otherwise, pay to have it prepared for you, but be satisfied that it is an accurate depiction of you, and that it does you justice!

CHAPTER III

STEP TWO:

MARKETING STRATEGIES

CHAPTER III

Step Two: Marketing Strategies

Plan your attack!

I hesitate for this to sound like a battle plan, but maybe that is a good analogy. At any rate, this must be as well-planned and organized as any military assault! Get out the armaments--that is, the supplies I listed in Chapter I; you will need them now.

In our case, the military assault becomes a marketing assault. Every company develops a strategy for getting their product or service in front of their buying public. Likewise, you will plan how to get your resume enough exposure to obtain interviews, the next step toward your new job.

The **Career Search System** includes eight source groups from which to develop your marketing plan. Depending on your background, you most likely will not need all eight, but if you do, the System is here is help! Each source works best for certain types or levels of applicants, and I have indicated that information at the beginning of the discussion of each source, under *"Pro's"* and *"Con's."* In addition, each source also has certain advantages and disadvantages, and those also are discussed.

Correctly utilized, these sources will provide as many interviews as you can handle. You may even find yourself in the enviable position of having too many interviews! In that case, be careful not to tire yourself and interview poorly. Two interviews per day is all most individuals can handle successfully.

First, you need to organize. Read through all eight sources and decide which ones you will use and in what time frame. Set up a weekly timetable or calendar in your notebook and schedule your time. This organization is more important than you think, so don't short-cut. Use the example on the following page, or one similar.

Sunday	Monday	Tuesday	Wednesday	Thursday	Friday	Saturday	Next Week
Read Ads. Prepare resume for mailing.	Call personnel agcys. Work on Direct Contacts	Attend trade assoc. meeting Interview w/ pers. agencies	Research ABC Corp.	Network Day Practice interviews.	Interview w/ ABC Corp @ 10:30 More network	Follow-up on interview w/ ABC Corp	Trade Assoc. meeting Tues. XYZ Corp interview Wed.

Sample—Weekly Timetable

Source #1: Direct Contact

Pro's: Works best for entry- and mid-level positions, especially for applicants with less than six or seven years of experience. Ideally suited for recent grads and first job changers, and persons seeking a specific industry or company. Good approach for individuals with specific experience and knowledge in one industry.

Con's: Labor intensive, especially in locating hiring authorities. Less effective for applicants with extensive experience that is not in one industry.

First of all, don't waste your time and money by blindly contacting or sending a resume to companies that hire only one or two employees each year. There are other sources to these companies, such as personnel agencies, newspaper ads, networking, etc. Use your time wisely, and concentrate your direct contact efforts on the companies that regularly hire for your specialty, or an industry that can use your specific experience. Unlike other books that are hardly more useful than the Yellow Pages, the Career Search System has researched the hiring practices of hundreds of companies. The result of this research is a selected list of companies (Appendix C) that omits companies that seldom have personnel needs, in favor of targeting firms that do the most professional-level hiring--which incidentally, are not necessarily the companies with the largest numbers of employees!

From my personal experiences and through research, I have compiled a list of approximately 200 Atlanta companies, found in Appendix C, and followed by numerous cross-references. These companies were selected for diversity and for the number of applicants hired each year (most hire between 25 and 100+ professional-level employees). I have tried to include examples from as many industries and professions as possible, and you probably will be interested in many. My associates or I spoke with each of these companies personally, and thus, the information is current and accurate, according to their staffing specialists.

Scan through the list of companies, and using the highliter marking pen, mark those in which you have an interest and those that hire in your specialty. I have included a thorough description of their operations and hiring procedures, as well as the types of applicants frequently sought and whether the company seeks entry-level and/or experienced personnel.

Read through the company profiles and you will find practically any and every job description included many times. I doubt there is any discipline for which I have not included at least a dozen major hiring sources. Even we liberal arts majors will find ample listings!

Next, review the cross-references. If there are specific industries or professions that interest you or in which you have experience, these lists will provide you with companies to contact.

In addition to the large corporations included here, you may know of other companies that hire in your field or for your specialty. Plan to direct-contact them also.

Now comes the laborious part: In your notebook, list the companies you plan to contact. Leave several spaces between each one to include information as you go along. Ideally, you should speak with each company personally by phone, but that is not always possible. The company representative may not be available, or you may not have the time or facility, especially if you are currently employed. In these cases, you should mail a resume and include a cover letter. (The cover letter is explained in Chapter VI.)

Whom should I contact?[1]

This is a debatable question, with many career counselors giving one answer and personnel managers another. As with most debates, there are good reasons to support both sides.

Most, if not all, career counselors would suggest that you should make your initial company contact with a "hiring authority," that is, a department manager who has control over the personnel requirements in his/her department. One reason is that this person may have current or projected personnel needs that have not been requisitioned from Human Resources or Personnel Recruiting. Secondly, this manager will most likely be the ultimate decision-maker with whom you would eventually interview, and thus you are a step ahead by starting here. This logic

---

[1] Although the vogue designation for the generic term "Personnel Department" is now "Human Resources," not all companies use that name. In addition, larger companies will also have a separate Recruiting or Staffing specialty within Human Resources. Although there are definite distinctions, I have used these terms fairly interchangeably, and for our purposes here, that is adequate.

concludes that Personnel Departments are often another hurdle to pass, and should be by-passed when possible.

There are many reasons why Personnel Departments may not be aware of all the needs within their companies. Often times, a manager will have plans to add to or alter the department in the future, and if your background fits the need, he/she may consider going ahead with the change now. Also, some department heads prefer to hire direct, rather than using their recruiting staff, who may be busy with other assignments. Furthermore, some companies are very decentralized and encourage managers to conduct their own personnel search and hiring. There are many other reasons, too, more than we can discuss here.

Most personnel managers would disagree with those assumptions, and strongly feel that you should contact them first. It is their function within the company to interview and screen applicants, following federal and local statutes, as well as company policies and procedures, and these guidelines may be unknown to executives attempting to conduct their own hiring. These personnel professionals have been trained to interview carefully and thoroughly, and they should be more in-tune to the overall needs of the company, not just one department.

In addition, some department managers may find your contact a nuisance, and thus you will be off to a bad start. Personnel may feel you are trying to short-circuit them, and they too will be annoyed. And finally, some companies have a firm policy that all initial contacts with applicants must be with Personnel.

But perhaps the best reason for contacting Personnel is simply expedience. Large companies will have many department managers over your specialty, and you cannot expect to contact all of them. Also, you may not have the time or resources to trace all the hiring authorities within a company. In these cases, you must utilize the company's Personnel Department.

Although in my practice, I nearly always work with Personnel, I adhere more to the former reasoning. I understand Personnel's concerns, but tend to agree that it is better to contact a hiring authority, especially when you have a friend or contact within the company who can tell you whom to contact. (Of course, this person may also tell you that the company requires you to start with Personnel.) However, you can assuage Personnel by sending them a resume also, and note whom you have already contacted.

Procedure to follow

Regardless whom you contact, Personnel or a department manager, the procedure is the same. In Appendix C I have listed most of Atlanta's largest hiring companies, and the procedure to follow if you go through Personnel. Note that in the company list, I have indicated the Personnel contact by job title or department, not by name. This is because the interviewing authority frequently changes and you will lose valuable time trying to contact or sending a resume to the wrong person. It is useful, however, to know the name of the interviewing authority, and that is one of the purposes in calling the companies directly.

Many people have a fear of the phone, and if you are one of them, you need to get over it! Preparing and rehearsing what you plan to say on the phone will help, and here is the procedure to follow:

When the company receptionist answers your call, ask for the Whomever (the department or job title I indicated as the contact, or the department manager you are seeking). When Whomever's secretary answers, say, "Hello. My name is Whatever, and I am seeking a position in _____(or as a _____). May I speak with Whomever?" Most likely at this point, you will be instructed to send your resume, in which case ask for the name of the person to whom you should address it, and record the name in your notebook. Don't be upset, however, if you are not given the name; some companies have a policy forbidding the disclosure of employee names. In the remote possibility that you actually do get the opportunity to speak with Whomever, be prepared. This is your chance to make a positive impression, have a brief telephone interview and schedule a personal interview also! Thus, you already should have composed and rehearsed a brief summary of your qualifications; you may have only one minute of his/her time, so make it count.

Assuming you were instructed to mail your resume, you will also need to include a cover letter. Having already written your resume, writing this will be easy. Chapter VI is a thorough discussion of correspondence, especially cover letters and their different purposes and forms. Several examples are included in Appendix B.

In the closing paragraph of your cover letter, you will have said that you plan to telephone them in a few days. Definitely do so. You want to know if your resume was received or lost along the way, and if it has been reviewed. Does the company have an opening for someone with your credentials? Is it being routed to another department or department manager? Are there any questions they would like to ask or additional information they need? Record the results of your phone call in your notebook.

If it appears that they do have an interest or need for your background, offer to come for a personal interview, if this is possible for you. If you are talking with company's interviewer, you must be ready for this telephone interview. Prepare and practice your interviewing techniques in advance, and don't be caught by surprise.

Finally, you will recall that I suggested you contact department managers whenever possible; but this is not to say that you should ignore Human Resources or Recruiting. In fact, if you are told by the department manager that no opening currently exists, I suggest you also contact Personnel. Individual departments and their managers seldom keep a resume file, but Human Resources usually will, and another need for your background may arise later. Even if the department manager does request your resume, you may wish to send one to Personnel as well, especially if you do not hear back from this manager within a reasonable time period. This is because the manager may be too busy with other projects to consider you now, but there may be another opening somewhere else within the company. Also, just as the Personnel Department may not be aware of projected needs within other departments, those department managers may not be aware of upper management's plans.

In summary, don't look upon personnel departments as just another hurdle to be avoided whenever possible, but rather utilize them when necessary or expedient. They have a purpose within their companies, and you should make use of it!

Source #2:   Classified Advertisements

Pro's: Cheap and easy source of many listings, covering all disciplines and levels. Good place to start. Good source to locate personnel agencies, as well as companies not using agencies, and small companies with infrequent needs. Often quotes salary. Local companies can be quick interviews.

Con's: You can get lost in the crowd of responses. May be difficult to discern good opportunities.

For obtaining employment in Atlanta, the largest source of announced openings is contained in the classified ads section of the Sunday edition of *The Atlanta Journal-Constitution*. It is a "must" in your job search. If you are currently living in Atlanta, you probably already receive it; if not, here is the procedure to order a subscription:

In Atlanta, call 522-4141. You will be billed or you can charge the fee on a credit card.

Out of Atlanta, but in Georgia, call (800) 282-8790. Same procedure as above.

Out of Georgia, call (800) 241-1164, and ask for extension 5868. Subscription rate varies by location and you must pay in advance or charge to a credit card.

This Sunday section is by far the largest in the Southeast. Within the fifty or so pages of ads will be up to 10,000 job openings, advertised by both companies and personnel agencies. These openings are listed alphabetically, by job category (accountants, data processing, engineers, sales, etc.). Peruse the categories that apply to you, and circle in red the openings for which you plan to apply.

In deciding which ads to consider, keep in mind that if the ad sounds too good to be true, it probably is! The newspaper tries to screen its clients, but bogus or misleading ads sometimes slip by. Here is one clue:

if you call a company, and someone answers with the phone number and then refuses to reveal the company's name, hang up!

After you have finished scrutinizing the ads, cut out the company (not agency) ads you circled and tape them onto blank pages to put in your notebook. Leave lots of empty space beside the ads, to record your activity with them.

Next, cut out the agency ads. You may notice that one agency is advertising several jobs for which you will want to apply. Write the name of each agency at the top of a page and then tape the corresponding ads on the page. Leave space on the page to record activity with that agency.

Now go back to the company ads, and contact each one. If the company included its phone number and did not specifically forbid phone calls, I suggest you call them and ask if you can speak with someone regarding the opening. If you do get through to the interviewer, be prepared for an interview then. Thus, you must already have planned what you will say in order to obtain a personal interview. You may wish to refer to "Chapter IV: Interviewing Techniques" before calling.

Most likely, however, you will be instructed to mail your resume before you speak with anyone personally regarding the position. Politely ask to whom you should address the resume, and record the information in your notebook. This personal touch is optional, but some recruiters will note it. Don't be surprised, however, if the receptionist has been instructed not to give out that information.

Along with your resume, you will include a cover letter. Refer to Chapter VI for a description and to Appendix B for illustrations. In your notebook, record the date you sent your resume, when you called to follow-up and the results.

Responding to personnel agency advertisements will be slightly different, and after reading the next section on Personnel Agencies, you will better understand the distinctions. Whenever possible, call them before sending a resume. By talking with them first, you can ascertain if you fit their available openings and whether or not that particular agency will be able to help you. Operating procedures vary from agency to agency, some requiring that you send a resume first, others requesting you to come in for a personal interview and bring your resume. If you are instructed to mail your resume, ask to whom you should address it and record that name in your notebook on the page for that agency. Some agencies will have several persons handling the same opening, and so there may not be a specific contact person.

It is not necessary to send a formal cover letter to agencies, although you may if it is convenient. Just a short typed or handwritten note with your salary requirements and restrictions (if any) is sufficient. Keep in mind, however, that this note is the agency's first impression of you and you must impress them in order to be referred to their client. Additional information on the use of this interview source in contained in the next section of this chapter.

Although *The Atlanta Journal-Constitution* is the largest source of classified ads, other local papers also have Sunday editions with classified ads. Two of these and their subscription phone numbers are as follows:

Marietta Daily Journal - (404) 428-9411

Gwinnett Daily News - (404) 963-0311

In addition to newspapers, another excellent source of classified ads is professional and trade magazines. If you have access to any periodicals in your field, review them and answer any classified ads that seem fruitful; these ads are usually on the last few pages of the publication. Respond to them as you would a newspaper ad. This source is especially helpful in determining which personnel agencies specialize in your field, because they are the ones that would place advertisements in specific journals.

If you have mailed your resume to a company, plan to call them in a few days to confirm that your resume was received. Ask if there are questions or additional information needed to complete your application. And, of course, offer to come for an interview at their convenience.

Just as you would prepare for a face-to-face interview, be ready for a phone screening also. Telephone interviews are usually short and cover only basic information. Typical questions will revolve around why you are seeking new employment and if you have the background needed for the job. If you pass this quick test, you will be invited for an interview.

A final word on classified ads, and this applies to direct contact and personnel agencies as well. A personal, face-to-face interview is always preferable to indirect contact, regardless how good your resume looks. Thus, whenever possible, try to be seen, rather than just heard. If you are very interested in a specific position and have been able to speak with a company interviewer on the phone, press for an interview time or at least offer to bring by your resume in person. And if you do deliver your resume in person, ask to simply meet the interviewer, if he/she is available.

Source #3: Personnel Agencies

Pro's: Probably the largest source of job openings. Easy and convenient. Good agencies will supply you not only with interviews, but also information on the company, the job and the interviewer. Can work well at all levels and fields. Usually free. Good source for quick interviews.

Con's: Not usually successful for hard-to-place applicants. Not easy to find most useful agencies. Fee sometimes involved, especially at lower-level openings.

The number of job openings represented collectively by the various personnel agencies in Atlanta can be numbered in the tens of thousands. There are literally hundreds of these agencies in Atlanta--more than twenty pages in the Southern Bell Yellow Pages and in at least three different listing categories! Because they represent so many companies and opportunities, they should be an invaluable source for you. Oftentimes, this industry receives a lot of bad press, much of it deservedly so. Some of these firms are excellent and do a very creditable job, and thus they are highly regarded and utilized by their client companies. But unfortunately, some agencies are downright awful. How do you select one?

First of all, don't select one; select several. Every agency would like to have you as its exclusive applicant, but it is in your best interest not to "put all your eggs in one basket," and to make yourself available to whichever ones can offer you exposure to the best companies and positions.

Understand, too, that every agency specializes in a certain level (entry, middle management, executive, etc.) or areas (clerical, management, engineering, etc.), and there are probably personnel agencies or individuals within an agency that specialize in your field. Your task is to zero in on the ones that handle applicants at your level and in your field of specialty.

In selecting the agencies you will contact, use this criteria:

1) Read the Sunday "Want Ads," especially in *The Atlanta Journal-Constitution*, and don't bother with the weekday ads, which are

mostly clerical. Pick out the agencies that are advertising the positions that interest you, and contact three or four.

2) Network. Ask friends which agencies they used and the results.

3) Contact the employment managers of major corporations and ask which agencies they use or would recommend.

4) If you graduated from a local college, check with the Career Placement Department, and ask for recommendations. In addition, you can call the university's academic department that covers your background, and ask if they are aware of agencies that specialize in your field.

5) Call the Atlanta Better Business Bureau at 688-4910 to inquire if there are complaints about any agencies in general, or specifically about the one(s) you may be considering.

Once you have selected the agencies you plan to contact, follow this procedure. If you are in Atlanta, you should visit them personally for two reasons:

1) to determine if they can adequately represent you or if you want them to represent you, and

2) to make a personal impression on them, so they can better present you to their clients.

If you are not local, call them to see if they can help you. If you are asked to send in a resume, do so, and then call back in a few days to check on the activity in your behalf. Ask them frankly if they will be able to arrange interviews and in what time frame. Be polite, but persistent. Can they help you or are you wasting your time? When would they like for you to call again? Do they have any suggestions for you?

Types of personnel agencies: Understanding the nature of personnel agencies and how they work will enable you to better utilize their services. Most importantly, realize that they are not philanthropic organizations; they are in business to make a profit. Their income is derived entirely from fees collected through their efforts at matching applicants with client companies.

Agencies can be broadly categorized into three groups, related to the sources of their income. Executive search firms, sometimes called "headhunters," are retained by companies to search for specific personnel

49

needs and are paid in advance by the retaining company. Since they work on a limited number of specific cases, they are not a good source to direct-call.

Temporary agencies derive their income from providing companies with contract labor, for which the company pays the agency and the agency in turn pays the laborers. Usually this is for hourly or clerical work, but some firms offer long-term contracts, especially for engineers and other specialized work. There are also temporary agencies specializing in short-term professional-level openings, especially in accounting and data processing. Many times these temporary positions will become permanent, so I suggest that if you are unemployed and have extra time, you may wish to consider applying to these agencies.

By far the largest number of agencies falls into the third group, called "contingency agencies," and these will be your best source to call. These firms are paid only when one of their applicants accepts employment through their efforts with one of their client companies, and thus, their fee is contingent upon making the placement. These agencies will have many job openings in many diverse industries, and with many different companies, many of whom may also have listed the same opening with other agencies.

Remember that since they are paid only when they make a job placement, they are most interested in applicants who fit the current needs of their clients, and if you are more difficult to place than another applicant, you will not get as much attention. When talking with them, state your employment objective, but be as flexible as possible and listen to their suggestions. However, you are under no obligation to accept any interview that does not meet your standards.

Interview with the agency as though it is the company with whom you hope to be employed, since you must impress them enough to get referred on to their clients. Many companies have established a strong rapport with the agency(s) they use, and thus have great confidence in the agency's opinion. At the end of your interview, ask how soon you can expect to hear from them and when you will be sent on an interview. Also, seek their frank appraisal of your resume and interviewing skills, and ask if they have any interviewing tips for you to consider.

During this interview, you should ask questions that will help you to evaluate the agency, the agency interviewer and the assistance they can offer you. Personnel agencies have notoriously high employee turnover, and it is not unlikely that this interviewer has been at the job for only a very short while. If this is the case, his/her opinion of your resume and interviewing skills may be totally useless! In addition, he/she may not understand your background and experience, and will not be able to present you to potential clients.

If the agency requires you to sign a contract, read it carefully before you sign and be sure to get a copy. Agency contracts are fairly standard, and generally speaking, you need not worry about signing one. The important facts to know are these:

1) You do not have to accept any offer extended unless you are sure it is what you are seeking. Do not allow the agency to pressure you into accepting a position you do not want.

2) No fee is involved until you do accept employment as a result of their service.

3) Before you accept a position through a personnel agency, be certain you understand your legal liability, if any, to the agency. For example, are there any circumstances under which you may be held responsible for all or part of the fee? Are you required to remain with the company for a period of time before your liability to the agency expires?

Lastly, a word about agency fees. Most professional-level personnel agencies handle only positions in which the hiring company pays the agency's fee. These are called "fee paid" positions and cost you nothing. I strongly recommend that you restrict your initial agency contacts to those handling only "fee paid" openings. If necessary, you can call the other agencies later.

Summary

Personnel agencies can be an excellent source and you should use them when possible, but recognize they do have limitations. If you are seeking employment in a very narrow field (*e.g.*, public relations or staff marketing), they likely will be of little help. If there is something in your background that makes you less marketable than their other applicants, you will not have good results with them. As I stated before, the best approach with agencies is to ask for a frank analysis of the help they can offer you.

I frequently speak with applicants who have been offended by a personnel agency--not that they were really mistreated, but rather they were made to feel like one of the herd, impersonal and dehumanized. Instead of "good-bye," they wanted to say "moo" or "baa"! Perhaps their interview was cold, short and perfunctory, or frequently interrupted. Another major complaint I often hear is that phone calls were not returned promptly, or even at all!

I won't make excuses for this behavior on the part of agencies, but I will explain why it happens, and I even will admit some guilt myself. Remember back to the resume chapter when I stated that I often receive up to 100 or so responses per advertisement. Then you must understand that each personnel agent will be handling many, many applicants at all times. Unfortunately, we often do not have enough time to please everyone and still do our work!

So don't let yourself be offended to the point of cutting yourself off from any possible source of leads and interviews. Your purpose is to use the agencies for your benefit, and don't lose sight of that objective, regardless of how you may feel toward the agency. I assure you that they mean no personal affront.

And remember, this source is only one of the many you have available. Don't make the mistake of waiting for an agency to find you a job when you have other sources to tap.

Source #4: Networking

Pro's: Most effective source overall. Works well for all experience levels, especially middle level. Best source for individuals changing fields, re-entering work force or other difficult-to-place situations.

Con's: Slow, time-consuming, labor intensive, lots of "dead-end" leads.

Looking at all the "con's" to networking might make you want to skip it, in favor of the easier and simpler methods. Before you do, consider this: More people find their jobs through networking than through any other source, at least 70%, and I have heard estimates of up to 85%! Perhaps this is a good example of the old adage, "You get what you pay for," because even though it is the most difficult, it is the most productive overall.

Just this morning, I spoke with a relative who has a friend whose neighbor was seeking an accounting management position. My relative has a client whom he heard was looking for someone in accounting, although he did not know the level of the position open. My relative told his friend who told his neighbor who called the client, and . . . well, to make this confusing story short, Fred is now the Accounting Manager at a large Atlanta-based trade association! Even if you did not follow that story line at all, you can get the idea of what "networking" is all about. Networking for a job is locating and using one source that leads you to other sources that result in a job. Or more simply, networking is using a source to a source.

Networking can take other forms. The example I cited was a referral to a company, but it could also be a referral to a personnel agency or some other third party that can get you an interview for an opening. Or it can be a source to a source to a source to a source, *ad nauseum*. If the referral is to a company or agency, treat it as you would a direct contact or personnel agency source, except you may mention the name of the person who referred you (with his/her permission, of course).

Although there are many organized network groups, two of which I am including here, most networking is simply done by word of mouth. Call your friends and ask for suggestions. When at parties, listen out for people who might be able to lead you to a source. Call the appropriate academic department head at a college and ask for suggestions. If possible, discuss your situation with clients and business associates.

A major source of leads and contacts can be found through professional trade associations. If you are already a member of a society that covers your field, you should definitely contact the president or job coordinator. If you are contemplating a career change, these groups can be a tremendous help. Search out the one(s) that pertain to your newly chosen field, contact them and attend their meetings. In doing research on this subject, I encountered many persons who obtained their jobs by networking at these monthly meetings, and thus I strongly urge you to try it also. This source is discussed in more detail in the next section, "Source #5: Professional and Trade Associations," and Appendix E includes information of many of the most active of these groups.

As you see, networking has infinite possibilities. Think about it, and you will surely come up with many more potential sources for contacts.

But don't expect instant results or that all you leads will be productive. In the case above, my relative referred his friend's neighbor to me also, but I had nothing available for someone with his background at the time. Thus, realize that although most of your leads will be unproductive, you must follow through on all of them. That is the slow, time-consuming part of networking. Don't let all the dead ends depress you; sooner or later, one or more of your leads will bear fruit.

Network Groups

In addition to your own network efforts, there are organized groups whose purpose is to help job seekers network. Listed below is information on two large public network groups in Atlanta, the Atlanta Job Network and Atlanta Exchange, Inc. I am also including information on the private Southeast Employment Network, a corporate network group.

The Atlanta Job Network is a non-profit, loosely structured group that meets weekly and welcomes anyone seeking a job, regardless of experience or background. At any given weekly meeting, you may be introduced to top executives, blue-collar workers, recent college graduates, and everything in between. There are no charges and no reservations. Their primary purpose is to help job seekers through

1) Support groups

2) Job networking

3) Seminars on the practical aspects of getting a job (*e.g.*, interviewing, resume preparation, focusing your job objective, planning a job search, etc.).

In addition, they maintain files of job openings sent to them by many metro employers, and these files can be perused at the weekly meetings.

In the past few months, I have spoken with many job-seekers who were very pleased with the assistance they received from this organization, and so I urge you to attend one or several of the meetings. There are six Job Network groups in the metro-Atlanta area, and you can meet with any one or more that you choose. Although they all meet in churches, they are non-sectarian. Telephone ahead for directions and to confirm times. You may also wish to inquire what topics are being discussed, and plan to attend the one(s) that would be most helpful to you.

-- St. Ann Catholic Church in Marietta. Meets every Tuesday at 8:00 pm. For direction, call 998-1373; for information ask for Sue Deering.

-- Corpus Christi Catholic Church in Stone Mountain. Meets every Monday at 7:30 pm. For directions, call 469-0395; for information, call John Humphries at 294-8377.

-- Immaculate Heart of Mary in northeast Atlanta. Meets every Thursday at 8:00 pm. For directions, call 939-0449; for information, ask for Jim Hammet.

-- St. Jude's Catholic Church in Sandy Springs. Meets every Monday at 7:30 and you must arrive early. For directions, call 394-8671; for information, call Jim Knocke at 393-4578. Oldest and largest of the Job Network groups; often has 150+ attendees! Offers specialized group discussions.

-- Roswell United Methodist Church in Roswell. Meets every Monday from 7:30 - 9:45. Also has Job Opportunity Bulletin Board, which lists current job openings; last year they had more than 300! For directions, call 993-6218; for information, ask for Marion Hix.

-- Peachtree Presbyterian Church in Buckhead. (Note: With 10,000 members, this is the largest Presbyterian church in the US.) Meets every Thursday at 7:30 in Room 237, and you are encouraged to arrive early for sign-in. Easy to find at 3434 Roswell Rd NW, but if you need directions, call the church office at 842-5800; for information on monthly topics, call Tim Lane at 434-0471.

The Atlanta Exchange is a predominantly black referral network, with 26 member organizations, representing many industries and professions. (Several of these are included in the appendix on Professional and Trade Associations.) They sponsor social gatherings, especially networking parties, and seminars on job hunting. An individual does not join the Exchange; instead, you call them, relay your background and experience, and they will refer you to a member organization that represents your industry or need. For more information or for the date of their next meeting, call Monica Chapman at 876-0490.

Southeast Employment Network

Unlike the other two network groups above, this is not an "applicant-oriented" network. Rather, it is a private group of 58± corporate MIS and systems engineering recruiters, who meet monthly to discuss the personnel needs of their individual companies and to share resumes they have received, as well as any other helpful recruiting information. There is no charge to applicants for this service. If your background or objective is computer systems-oriented, you can have your resume circulated to all 58± member companies simply by mailing one copy to

Mr. Dana Milner, c/o Ernst & Young

2100 Gas Light Tower, 235 Peachtree St NE, Atlanta, GA 30303. Or you can call him for more information at 581-1300.

Source #5: Trade and Professional Associations

Pro's: Works well for middle- and upper-level executives, and somewhat for entry-level. Good source for changing careers.

Con's: May be costly if you must join first or pay to attend meetings. Can be slow and time-consuming getting to the source.

Trade and professional associations were referred to in the preceding section on networking. Nevertheless, these organizations are so valuable that the topic merits separate consideration.

Few job seekers are aware of the excellent job referral services and training seminars offered by their professional associations. Although not all associations offer these services, those that do can be invaluable aids.

Association help comes in many ways, including monthly newsletters listing both job seekers and job openings, a resume bank retained for companies to peruse, a job information "hot line," and direct matching of jobs and applicants. Smaller organizations may have a less formal, yet very effective networking system. In addition, many associations sponsor career development seminars, covering such topics as job search within their industry, career planning, industry innovations, etc.

There is an organization covering virtually every conceivable job description, industry or academic discipline. Although you already may be a member of one or more of these associations, there likely are other associations of which you may not be aware, but from which you could benefit. *National Trade and Professional Associations of the United States* (published by Columbia Books, Inc., Washington, DC) is a catalogue that lists 6,200 trade and professional associations and labor unions with national memberships. This book is available at most public libraries, and it includes not only addresses and descriptions of each organization, but a cross reference section to access associations by subject. You likely will be surprised to learn that many disciplines are represented by numerous associations, some of which specialize in specific industries. For example, under the heading "Marketing," there are 75+ specialty associations, in addition to the 49,000-member American Marketing Association! Thus, I urge you to incorporate this publication in your job search. (If you are not able to obtain this through a local public library, mail order information is included in "Source #8: Publications.")

Nearly all of the largest associations offer job assistance on the national level. Moreover, I have researched a number of these groups that offer some sort of job assistance locally, either formal or informal, and included them in Appendix E. If your association is not listed, I suggest that you contact the national headquarters of your association and ask for the local Atlanta chapter president, and then inquire about their direct career assistance, if any. Even if they do not have any formal set-up, remember that you can attend their meetings and network; in fact, I have recently spoken with several persons who obtained their current jobs that way! In future editions, I hope to add many more associations, and I would appreciate hearing from you if you have information on others that are not included in my current list.

In some cases, you must be a member of the association offering employment assistance before they will help you. However, I was pleased to find that many organizations are more interested in helping an applicant secure employment now, assuming he/she will join the association later. Since membership dues can be expensive--prohibitively so if you are unemployed--I suggest you call the association contact I have listed to inquire if membership is a prerequisite.

Some associations require a small fee to cover costs, especially if their services are extensive or staffed by volunteers. In some cases, the fee is waived for members. I have noted these charges and other requirements when applicable.

In addition to the direct help these organizations offer, you can help yourself too, by attending their meetings and networking there. Most associations meet monthly and welcome visitors and potential members, as well as current members. Again, there may be a fee involved or reservations required, so check ahead. Appendix E also includes information on monthly meeting dates.

Once there, meet as many members as possible, and seek their help and advice. Take a small, pocket-size note pad to record leads and other information, and be certain you take several resumes to hand out.

In reviewing Appendix E, Trade and Professional Associations, you will note that I often have included names to contact, rather than titles, as I did in the company list. This is because many organizations are mostly volunteer and not listed in the phone book, and the fastest way to reach them is through a member or office. However, since these officials are usually elected for one year only, you may be referred to the current slate of officers for help.

I personally know of many people who found their jobs through associations, and so I am positive it works. Definitely plan to incorporate it in your search. In your notebook, record the names of the associations you contact, the people with whom you speak and the results. These contacts will be helpful now and later.

After you are employed, I strongly urge you to become active in your association. The knowledge you will gain from the meetings, programs and seminars will be very helpful in advancing your career. Drawing from your own experiences, you can also be very helpful to other job seekers--and then too, you never know when you might need their services again!

Source #6:   Government

Pro's: Stable and secure. Local and state jobs are generally permanent Atlanta. Many openings for recent grads.

Con's: Can be very long and complex procedures. Not good source if you need a job quickly, although efforts are underway to streamline federal hiring.

There are more than 200,000 government employees in metro-Atlanta, and that figure is increasing at almost 5% annually! (Source: Georgia Department of Labor) The approximate numbers are these:

Federal - 45,200 (including 6,000 in defense)

State - 42,000 (15,000 in education and 27,000 other)

Local (18-county MSA) - 122,500 (approximately one-half in education).

Appendix F includes addresses and contact data divided into the above three groups.

If at all possible, I suggest you go to one of the five local Georgia State Employment Offices listed below, where you will find not only Georgia openings, but many federal and local job lists as well. Call if you need directions:
-- Clayton County: 1193 Forest Pkwy, Lake City, GA; (404) 363-7643
-- Atlanta: 2811 Lakewood Ave SW, Atlanta; (404) 669-3300
-- Dekalb County: 1275 Clarendon Ave, Avondale Estates, GA; (404) 288-1345
-- Cobb County: 2972 South Cobb Dr SE, Smyrna, GA; (404) 434-6303
-- Gwinnett County: 1535 Atkinson Rd, Lawrenceville, GA (404) 995-6913

If you are not in Atlanta or unable to go to one of the above offices, then

(1) go to your local US Office of Personnel Management (or in smaller cities, the State Employment Services Office) and request the Federal Job Opportunities List for Atlanta (out of state, ask for Georgia and peruse for Atlanta openings);

(2) write the Georgia State Merit System and request the pamphlet, "The State Employment Process" (address included in merit system discussion in this chapter);

(3) contact the local government offices listed in Appendix F.

U. S. (Federal) Government

The process for obtaining a federal job is somewhat complex, and that is why I urge you to go to your local State Employment Services Office, including the five in Atlanta. They should be able to explain the procedures involved and help you with the applications.

Most federal government agencies hire through the Office of Personnel Management (OPM), formerly known as the civil service commission, and a competitive exam is required. This exam may be all written, all experience-oriented, or a combination of both. You can obtain information on application procedures, application forms and the Federal Job Opportunities List for Atlanta at many locations, including the employment offices in all states, college placement departments, and the offices of all members of Congress. These sources will be the fastest methods of obtaining the information, but if none of these sources is available to you, you can write the OPM Atlanta Area Office and request application information and the Federal Job Opportunities List to be mailed to you. I am told this office is extremely busy, and thus use the alternate sources when possible. Their address here is

U S Office of Personnel Management
Atlanta Area Office
75 Spring St SW, Suite 956
Atlanta, GA 30303-3309.

Do _not_ call. All requests for information must be in writing.

If you are in Atlanta, the fastest and simplest method to learn of the application procedures and job openings is to visit the self-service Federal Job Information Center, open Monday through Friday, from 9 - 4. They are located at 75 Spring St SW, and you can review the job list in Room 960.

Certain federal organizations fill their job vacancies through their own hiring systems, and have no contact with OPM. The largest of these in Atlanta is the US Postal Service (USPS), with more than 7,000 employees here, including some 3,000 at the managerial level. Interestingly, nearly all USPS employees start as clerks or carriers, and only the highest levels are hired from outside the system. Thus, one would start entry-level, and then bid for higher-level positions after one year of employment. Numerous college grads are hired each year into this program. Call (404) 765-7234 for information on job vacancies, then fill out an application and you will be notified when to take the exam required of all applicants.

Another federal agency conducting its own hiring is the General Accounting Office (GAO), a Congressional agency and not under the Executive Branch. Most of their hiring is for economics, public administration, accounting/finance and computer-related degrees, both entry-level and experienced. A job announcement is published each fall, and applications are taken from September through April. They also offer several co-op programs and summer internships. Call (404) 331-6900 for information.

In addition to the above organizations and procedures, there exist two alternative and usually faster methods of obtaining entry-level federal employment, GS 5 - 7 levels, currently filled mostly by recent college graduates with good grade point averages (GPA's).

PAC Authority: At the beginning of 1990, there exists a system called "PAC authority," and it enables certain agencies to hire for specified positions, called Professional and Administrative Career trainee positions, directly from the outside, instead of utilizing OPM. This system will be changing, probably in the second quarter of 1990, and the new system has not been finalized at this writing. However, it appears that the new authority will be similar to the existing, except it will rely on several factors, including college GPA and/or a written examination, in lieu of a high GPA.

Outstanding Scholar Authority: A part of the PAC authority, this program will continue in existence, although the GPA stipulations may be modified. Recent graduates with a GPA of 3.5+ (on a 4.0 scale) or who have graduated in the top 10% of their class, can be hired directly from the outside, bypassing OPM.

Unfortunately, there is no central list of which agencies are or will be involved and/or when, so you must contact each one and inquire if they have available any Outstanding Scholar or PAC openings (or whatever the new system will be called). The largest federal agencies in Atlanta and their addresses are included in Appendix F. My contact at OPM also suggests that you first write OPM, indicating your objectives and qualifications, and they will send you information regarding the agencies that may have openings for you. At the same time, you can ask about the new system replacing PAC.

Incidentally, the federal government offers its employees alternate work schedules, one of which allows an employee to work nine-hour days, Monday - Thursday, and then have Friday afternoon free! It's still a 40-hour week, but the half-day can make a nice, long weekend! This schedule is also finding favor within the private sector as well, and I have noted in Appendix C (the list of companies) some of those that also offer this benefit.

State of Georgia

The vast majority of state job vacancies are filled through the Georgia Merit System, which last year hired more than 5,000. If you are in Atlanta, again I refer you to the state employment offices for information on current openings. A list of available openings is published each Friday and is available at all Georgia state agencies and colleges, as well as the labor departments of all states. It cannot be obtained by writing or calling; rather, you must go in person to an employment office or to the merit system office, located in the same building as the MARTA Georgia State station. However, you can call (404) 656-2724 for a recorded announcement of the hiring procedure. Their address is
    State of Georgia Merit System
    200 Piedmont Ave, Suite 418, West Tower, Atlanta, GA 30334.

The merit system office is open Monday - Friday, 8 - 4:30, but you are encouraged to arrive by 3:00.

One of the larger non-merit system agencies is the Department of Audits. It is divided into two sections, financial and performance, whose addresses are listed in Appendix F.

Local Governments

Appendix F lists the contact data and procedure followed by the five major metro counties, plus the City of Atlanta.

Source #7:   Public Agencies

Pro's: Free and easy source. Free testing and counseling available. Listings at all level levels of experience. Includes jobs available in the public and private sectors.

Con's: Companies tend to shy away from public agencies, since there is limited applicant screening or matching.

Georgia Employment Service

The state-operated employment service has five offices in metro Atlanta, and maintains lists of job openings from corporations, the Georgia State Merit System and many federal agencies. In addition, they offer information on the procedure to follow in applying for state and federal government positions. At your request, a trained counselor will administer and evaluate a battery of aptitude tests (up to 4 1/2 hours long!) and occupational interest tests.

You must go to an office in person (do not mail a resume) and have your Social Security card and valid driver's license to use for identification. Office hours are 9 a.m. - 4:30 p.m., Monday thru Friday. A brief orientation session is required first and is given at several different times during the day at each location; call and ask the times before you go to an office. Here are the five branches, so pick the one closest to you. Call if you need directions.
   -- Clayton County: 1193 Forest Pkwy, Lake City, GA; (404) 363-7643
   -- Atlanta: 2811 Stewart Ave SW (corner of Stewart and Lakewood Ave), Atlanta; (404) 669-3300
   -- DeKalb County: 1275 Clarendon Ave, Avondale Estates, GA; (404) 288-1345
   -- Cobb County: 2972 S. Cobb Drive SE, Smyrna, GA; (404) 434-6303
   -- Gwinnett County: 1535 Atkinson Rd, Lawrenceville, GA; (404) 955-6913

Georgia State University

The state-supported colleges and universities of Georgia have Career Placement Departments that are open to the public, with certain restrictions. Atlanta's largest university, Georgia State University, maintains an extensive computerized file of applicants that is available to interested employers. Although most of these applicants are recent grads, I am told that they also receive calls almost daily from prospective employers seeking experienced personnel! If you are enrolled at Georgia State or you are an alumnus(a), call 651-2380 to be included in their placement services. If you are neither, you must have a letter from your college, stating job placement reciprocity. Send that letter, your resume and a cover letter requesting that a "Placement File" be opened for you in a certain field (accounting, sales, engineering, etc.). Once you are approved, usually within three days, you are entered into their computer, to be notified of positions available in your field. Further, your resume will be kept on file for prospective employers to peruse. Send the required information to

Mr. Ben Upchurch, Director of Placement
Georgia State University, University Plaza, Atlanta, GA 30303.
Or for more information, call (404) 651-3617.

Professional Placement Network

The Georgia Department of Labor has offered this service since 1986, but I suspect it is still not well-known. The Professional Placement Network (PPN) publishes a monthly newsletter which is circulated to more than 750 active Atlanta employers, and includes resume synopses of 130 job-seekers, divided into job categories (accounting, engineering, advertising, etc.). The newsletter includes only college graduates with at least two years experience, although a few recent grads are sometimes included (3.0 GPA required). The synopses published are assigned a code number for anonymity, and interested employers can contact the PPN to get a full resume, with the approval of the applicant.

This service is becoming more recognized and utilized, and currently the PPN receives requests for more than 175 resumes each month from employers responding to the newsletter! In addition to the newsletter, they maintain a resume file for employers to peruse or call for potential applicants.

Important: the newsletter has room for only approximately 130 synopses, although they receive many more than that number of applicants. They screen out the synopses that are poorly written or unqualified, and they look for advanced degrees and other examples of over-achievement. (All resumes received are kept in the resume file, however.) Thus, the quality of your synopsis is important.

To obtain an application form, call or write
Mr. James Coggins,

Georgia Department of Labor, 2811 Lakewood Ave SW, Atlanta, GA 30315.
(404) 669-3327

Southeast Employment Network

I also discussed this group under Source #4: Networking. This is a private group of 58± corporate MIS and systems engineering recruiters, who meet monthly to discuss the personnel needs of their individual companies and to share resumes they have received, as well as any other helpful recruiting information. There is no charge to applicants for this service. If your background or objective is computer systems-oriented, you can have your resume circulated to all 58± member companies simply by mailing one copy to

Mr. Dana Milner, c/o Ernst & Young

2100 Gas Light Tower, 235 Peachtree St NE, Atlanta, GA 30303.
Or you can call him for more information at 581-1300.

Source #8: Publications

Pro's: Sources smaller, specialized companies for specific industry experience, as well as larger corporations and employers. Most helpful for experienced applicants searching for companies in their industry.

Con's: Moderate expense, some duplication from other sources.

I am including information on reference material that you may wish to order and some comments regarding each. In contacting the companies that are included in these publications, treat them as a Direct Contact.

Atlanta Chamber of Commerce

Several helpful publications are available from the Atlanta Chamber of Commerce. (Prices subject to change.) Write and send check to
P O Box 1740, Atlanta, GA 30301.
Attn: Public Information Dept.

1) Atlanta City Map - $1.00

2) Fortune 500 - Lists the Fortune 500 firms in the Atlanta area. Most are included here in Appendix C. $2.00

3) Headquartered Firms - Lists alphabetically the firms headquartered in metro Atlanta. The largest are included in Appendix C. $3.00

4) Larger Employers - Lists firms with 300+ total employees in Atlanta. Many of these are also included in Appendix C. $2.00

5) Manufacturing Directory - Lists more than 1500 manufacturing firms in metro Atlanta, including Standard Industrial Classifications. Good source to locating companies in your manufacturing specialty. $15.00

6) Newcomer Employment Package - Includes the Newcomers Guide, Employment Services and Larger Employers publications. Good start if you are not local.

7) Atlanta High Tech Manufacturers - Lists 200 such firms, taken from the larger Manufacturing Directory. If you have a high tech background or interest, this publication is probably enough, and cheaper. $2.00

Multi-national Corporations

If you are interested in foreign companies with facilities in Atlanta, order the *Georgia International Facilities* book. This 125-page book includes information on the 34 countries with Georgia operations, plus the consulates, trade offices and chambers of commerce of each country. Currently there is no charge for this major publication! Order from
Georgia Department of Industry and Trade, Research Division
230 Peachtree Street, P O Box 1776, Atlanta, GA 30301.

Book of Lists

The *Atlanta Business Chronicle* produces an annual publication called the *Book of Lists*, which includes the 25 or so largest companies in various categories, and information about their sales, number of employees, major clients, etc. It is interesting reading in general, and it could be helpful to you to locate companies within a specific industry or profession. The 1989 edition lists 45 categories, including accounting firms, architectural/engineering firms, auto dealerships, banks, travel agencies, ad and PR agencies, computer companies, credit unions, HMO's, hospitals, hotels, law firms, printers, telecommunications companies, real estate firms and agents, plus many more. To order, send $11.95 (includes postage and handling) to
Atlanta Business Chronicle
1801 Peachtree St NE, Suite 150, Atlanta, GA 30309.

National Trade and Professional Associations of the United States

I made reference to this catalogue in "Source #5: Professional and Trade Associations." It is available at most public libraries, but you may order it if you wish. Send $48.00 (postpaid) to
Columbia Books, Inc., Publishers
1350 New York Ave NW, Suite 207
Washington, DC 20005-3286.

CHAPTER IV

STEP THREE:

INTERVIEWING TECHNIQUES

CHAPTER IV

Step Three: Interviewing Techniques

Congratulations! The fact that you are being given an interview indicates that you obviously have presented yourself well so far and that the interviewer has at least some interest in you to grant you some of his/her time. You have worked hard to get to this point, but don't let up yet.

Preparation

Like a good Boy/Girl Scout, "Be Prepared." This is absolutely essential to a successful interview. In fact, you should never interview without some prior research. Nervous? That could be because you haven't adequately prepared! Being prepared not only settles the stomach, it impresses the interviewer as well.

Research the company, and when possible, research the job and interviewer. Learn as much about the company as timely possible, but don't feel that you must know more than the interviewer. Here is the basic information to digest:

-- Most importantly, know the company's products or services. What do they offer, provide, manufacture or sell?

-- What is their annual growth and how profitable are they?

-- What can you find out about their industry in general, including competitors?

-- What is their ranking within their industry?

-- Research the company's history.

-- Try to determine their reputation. Are they considered aggressive? What is their personnel turnover rate? How are they regarded by their customers? This information is subjective and may be difficult to obtain, but if you have a reliable source, it is good information to know.

-- Find out as much as you can about the interviewer(s), especially background and previous employment, interviewing techniques, hobbies, interests, etc. If your interview was arranged through an intermediary, that person may be able to relay good insight into the whims of the interviewer(s); good personnel agencies should always have this information.

Researching most of the company data is easy, and there are many sources. The simplest method is to call the company and ask for an annual report to be mailed to you. If the company declines, as most privately-held companies will, or if you are short on time, go to your college placement center or the public library. Some good reference books include Standard and Poor's, Moody's, Million Dollar Directory, American Corporate Families and Thomas Register. All these are readily available on the second floor at the Atlanta-Fulton County Library downtown (Take MARTA to Peachtree Center station; exit Ellis Street and then West Peachtree escalator).

Networking is also a good source. Ask friends or business contacts if they are familiar with the company; however, keep in mind you may be hearing biased information or rumor, and treat this information accordingly. If you know some of the company's clients, you can carefully and discreetly call them for information.

Anticipate certain questions and be ready with your answers. I recently spoke with a Vice President of Human Resources who told me that for his last job search, he wrote down fifty questions an interviewer might ask. Then he wrote down his answers, and put it aside for a few days. Reading them later, he realized how bad some of his answers really were, and he thought them through again. That took a lot of time--but then too, his thoroughness paid off in a big way!

72

It is impossible to anticipate every question you might be asked, but knowing what your interviewers are seeking with their questions will help you plan your responses. Of course, you must have the technical expertise required for the position. Excluding that, interviewers look for three primary factors:

1) Clear and certain job focus. You know what job you are currently seeking and how it fits into your career plans.

2) Your life patterns--that is, demonstrated patterns of success, accomplishment, over-achievement, etc., and the opposites.

3) Your ability to "sell yourself"--that is, convincing the interviewer you are the one to hire! In my experiences, more applicants are rejected for failing this, than for any other reason.

The following characteristics are ones most often rated by an interviewer. Read these through several times, and think how they may be asked to you and how you will respond to best "sell yourself."

Intelligence: Conceptual ability, breadth of knowledge, verbal expression, organized thoughts, analytical thought process, logical decision-making.

Decisiveness: Non-ambivalent, willing to commit self when asked, makes definite choices, lets you know where he/she stands on issues, not tentative.

Energy and Enthusiasm: Animated, spontaneous, fast-paced throughout, positive attitude.

Results-orientation: Responses revolve around task accomplishment, gets to the point, emphasizes achievements, provides information relevant to interview objectives, able to give specific instances and examples.

Maturity: Acceptance of responsibility for one's actions, poised, self-confident, appropriately dressed, general demeanor, relaxed, ability to reflect on experiences, understands one's strengths and weaknesses, clear career goals.

Assertiveness: Responds in a forceful manner, does not ramble, speaks in a convincing tone, persuasive, good at selling self and ideas, good communicator.

Sensitivity: Sincere, friendly, tactful, responsive, not aloof, listens as well as speaks, asks relevant questions.

Openness: Discusses short-comings as well as strengths, is not pre-occupied with saying the right thing, consistent responsiveness regardless of content.

Tough-mindedness: Stands up to interviewer when there is disagreement, discusses persons and events critically, does not allow emotions to cloud perceptions.

Interviewing Tips

Over the years, interview styles and questions have changed. Many years ago, the vogue questions were "What are your strengths?" and conversely, "What are your weaknesses?" Until recently, "Tell me about yourself" was the technique of choice. Although you will still encounter those questions, the current fad in interviewing now revolves around open-ended questions asking for specific examples or instances: "Give me an example of how you . . . ."

The following frequently asked questions include those three types, as well as many others you should anticipate:

1) How did you choose your college? Why did you choose your major? What did you intend to do with that degree?

2) Why did you leave your past employers?

3) Pick three adjectives to describe yourself.

4) Give me a specific example of a problem you overcame in your job.

5) What are the qualities of a good manager [salesperson, accountant, engineer, etc.]?

6) How would you rate your success with your job? Why were you successful?

7) What did you like [or dislike] most about your last job?

8) Rank these in order of preference: salary, location, nature of the job.

9) Where do you expect to be in your career in five years?

10) Tell me about yourself.

11) What do you consider the major accomplishment(s) or achievements(s) in your life and/or career?

12) Give me an example of an unpopular policy you had to implement and how you did it.

13) Why are your considering a job change?

14) Evaluate your present and past supervisors. (Recent grads may be asked to evaluate their instructors.)

15) Why haven't you found a job after so many months?

16) What interests you about this job?

17) What can you contribute to our organization?

18) How well do you communicate with others? Give me an example of a communications problem you encountered and how you solved it.

19) What constructive criticism have former bosses made to you, and what did you do in response?

20) If you were hiring for this position, what would you look for?

There are many "right" answers to those questions, and undoubtedly, there are just as many wrong ones! Before reading further, decide what your answers would be. If you have access to a tape or video recorder, record your answers now, and then review your performance. After you have read my suggested responses and reviewed your answers, repeat this exercise.

Here are some reasons behind the questions, and some suggestions for your consideration:

1) Even if you attended the University of Saint Playboy-in-the-Caribbean and majored in underwater basket-weaving, you must present a logical reason for doing so. Companies want to feel that you are and have been in control of your life, and that you made your decisions based on a logical career plan.

2) Never say anything derogatory about former employers. Rather, you left your previous employment for more responsibility, a greater challenge and a better career opportunity. If your departure was the result of a reduction-in-force, make that clear, and note that your position was not refilled.

3) This must be the oldest and simplest question of all, but it still amazes me how many applicants are stunned when I ask it! There are other ways of phrasing this question, such as "What are your strong points?" or "How would your best friend (or employer) describe you?" Remember, this is a business interview, so pick adjectives that are business-oriented. Unless you are pursuing a career in the Scouts, do not be "loyal, thrifty, brave, obedient, etc." Here are some good choices: aggressive, ambitious, assertive, self-motivated, goal-oriented, self-disciplined, persistent, good communicator, competitive, team player, etc. Having chosen your adjectives, now think of specific instances illustrating how you have used these qualities, and be prepared to relate them.

4) The interviewer is essentially asking you what you have accomplished in your job. Choose an achievement that best illustrates your results-orientation.

5) Obviously, you must exemplify the same qualities of a good whatever, so pick adjectives similar to the ones you chose in question #3. Then be prepared with several good illustrations.

6) Always rate yourself highly, but not perfect. Even if you were fired from your last job, you should rate yourself well. On a scale of one to ten, you should pick eight or nine. Why were you successful? Because you possess the qualities of a good whatever that you identified in questions #3 and #5.

7) Since you knew what your job would be, there must have been something about it that you liked, or why else would you have taken it? Thus, you should have many items about your job that you like, and only a few that you dislike, although these dislikes obviously outweigh the positive aspects of your job. Above all, do not blame your displeasure on any person, especially your supervisor; the interviewer will question your version of the conflict. Never make any references to location, personality conflicts or any answer that would allow the interviewer to conclude that you could be the problem.

Let me stress, however, that you should not attempt to sugarcoat your feelings about your present employment. If you are seriously considering a job change, then you must have serious misgivings about your job. You should discuss them frankly and forcefully, showing that you have given this considerable thought and have concluded that your talents would be best used elsewhere. Your thoughts here must be well-organized and logical, and expressed well enough to convince the interviewer.

Here are some simple suggestions, from which you can develop your answer: you feel that you are not "growing" in your current position; you would like to be better compensated for your contribution (especially good for salespersons); you want to assume more responsibility. Incidentally, note that these answers are positive in tone (versus, "I am not being adequately compensated....," etc.).

8) Another easy question, but frequently missed. Always have location last, even if you really don't mean it; companies need to think you are more interested in them and their position than you are in where you are located. Nature of the job should be first, except possibly in the case of commissioned salespersons.

9) This can be tough if you don't know the company's normal career path. Certainly you expect to have been promoted, perhaps more than once. I suggest you answer with a question such as, "I expect to have achieved at least one promotion, but I am not familiar with your company's career path for this position. What should I reasonably expect?" Do not give the impression that you expect too much too soon, and might become a disgruntled employee. And don't say you expect to be in the interviewer's position; that weak answer went out years ago!

10) I think this is the hardest question of all, and yet it also allows you to take control and direct the interview as you choose. Take this opportunity to stress accomplishments and achievements in your life and career, to describe yourself (the three adjectives again!) and to state your career aspirations. Show logical movements and decisions. This answer must sound organized, yet spontaneous.

11) Surely you must have thought about this many times, but I am always surprised at how often an applicant falls apart when this is asked. Here is your chance to really pat yourself on the back, and don't be shy!

12) This question was recently asked to one of my applicants applying for an personnel management position, and it could also be asked of many other positions. For example, if you are a salesperson, how do you tell your clients about an expected price increase? How do manufacturing managers explain increased productivity goals? Your answer will reveal much about your intelligence, results-orientation and sensitivity, so be prepared with a thoughtful answer.

13) As in question #2, you are leaving for more responsibility, challenge and opportunity. Here, however, you can add current considerations such as these: you are seeking a more dynamic or aggressive company; you want to use your knowledge and experience to transfer into a faster growing industry (avoid saying a more stable industry, which sounds as if you are running *away*, rather than *to*); you are seeking a company that will allow you more personal input into daily operations; you are seeking a company that gives more personal responsibility for final results. Again, do not denigrate your employer, past or present.

14) Here you are displaying your tough-mindedness and objectivity. Using specific examples, mention a few good and bad points about current or former bosses, and how you might have acted differently. Most of your supervisors were probably good, so be certain that your praise is greater than your fault-finding, lest you be considered too negative or possessing a "bad attitude." Also, do not be too derogatory and never personal--you are commenting on performance as a supervisor, not as a "person."

15) The standard reply is this: "Finding a job is easy; finding the right job takes a while longer." Quite likely, this will not satisfy the interviewer, and you may be asked for more details regarding your prolonged job search. Since this is essentially a negative discussion, try to end it as soon as possible, without getting defensive. If you have received job offers that you declined, explain why--with good, logical reasons, of course!

16) If you don't have a good answer to this question, your interview is over. Your preparation should have given you at least some information about the job, and you must show how your qualities match the nature of this job.

17) If you can't sell yourself now, you never will. From your preparation, you should already know how your background and experience will benefit them, so tell them now--be assertive and lay

78

it on thick! Show how their needs mesh closely with your own qualities, and include several examples.

18) Over the years, I have reviewed thousands of job requisition forms, and nearly all have listed good communicative skills as a requirement for the job. Spend some time reflecting on how well you communicate your thoughts and ideas, and have several examples ready that demonstrate your ability to overcome problems communicating with others (superiors, subordinates, peers, clients, etc.).

19) In other words, how well do you take criticism? This question is a variation of "What are your weak points?" or "What are your limitations?" If your answer is that you never have been criticized, then I think you are lying and so will the interviewer! Since we are all imperfect, we all have made mistakes and thus encountered criticism. You must freely and openly admit your shortcomings (but not too many and not too severe!) and give specific examples of what you have done to overcome them.

20) This is too easy. Describe yourself, using a variation of the adjectives you used in questions #3 and #6.

These twenty questions and answers are only a few of the many you might encounter, and I do recommend that you write down as many questions and your answers as you can. Then rehearse your answers aloud, perhaps to a friend for criticism.

Relocation

In addition to the above questions, you will undoubtedly be asked about your availability for relocation. How you handle the following questions can determine the result of your interview:

-- Are you available for immediate relocation?

-- Will you be open for relocation at a later date?

-- Does your spouse also have a career, and will relocation be a problem for him/her?[1]

-----

[1]Yes, this question is legal, although it must be carefully presented so it will not suggest sex discrimination. Usually, it

-- Are there any potential problems that could affect your relocation, now or in the future?

These are definitely some of the most important questions you will encounter during the interview. I know I may get redundant here, but I must emphasize the importance of how you handle this series of questions. It is paramount that the interviewer feel that your major concern is the job--its nature, responsibilities, scope and potential. Be careful that you say nothing that will give the interviewer the impression that location is more important, or even equally so. If you say anything that leads the interviewer to conclude that location will be a primary factor in your career, you likely will not be considered further.

Unless the company with whom you are interviewing has operations in only one location, you may be required to move to another locale, either now or later. Since restricting your geographic availability eliminates an infinite number of jobs for which you could be qualified, I strongly urge you to consider any relocation as just another part of the total package, and evaluate it accordingly. If you are happy with your job, you most likely will be happy regardless of the location. Plus, companies need to think you are promotable, which usually involves a transfer, even if you are then assigned in Atlanta. If you are just starting your career, you may want to consider other Sunbelt locations, planning to request a transfer or promotion to Atlanta when one occurs. In fact, if you really like the company and its career path, that plan is a very viable alternative, especially if your company is Atlanta-headquartered.

On the initial, screening interview, companies sometimes decline to reveal the location of their opening, in order to determine your promotability/transferability. I have even had companies describe the position as requiring a relocation, even though it was for Atlanta! Furthermore, even if (or especially if) you know the position for which you are interviewing is in Atlanta, you should state your availability for relocation, so that the company will feel you are promotable.

Consequently, unless there are absolutely no circumstances under which you will consider relocation, I urge you to state that you are totally open for relocation, now as well as later. Should you receive a job offer in a location unacceptable to you, you can simply say no. But you will never have the opportunity to evaluate the whole offer, if your restrictions stop the interview process at the beginning.

---

will not be asked so straight-forwardly, but the information somehow will be gleaned.

Realistically, however, I realize that you may have a logical reason for your relocation restrictions, or even simply that you prefer to remain in Atlanta; after all, that is probably why you bought *ATLANTA JOBS*, and not Cleveland Jobs! From my own personnel experiences, I know that finding applicants who will relocate is perhaps the single greatest problem in job placement, and I suggest that most corporate recruiters would concur.

So if you don't want to relocate, how do you answer these questions? That depends on your reasons and how well you present them, although any reason will be viewed with suspicion.

A few years ago, I secured employment in Atlanta for an applicant whose child was in extensive therapy at Emory University Hospital, and thus he needed to remain here for the near future. That was an understandable reason, and the company wanted him badly enough to accept this, at least temporarily.

On the other hand, I have also interviewed hundreds, maybe thousands, of applicants (especially recent grads) who simply liked it here, and would not relocate. From a corporate standpoint, that's not a good reason, and again I urge you to reconsider, or at least come up with a better, more logical reason.

In between these two extremes are many valid cases for remaining in Atlanta. For example, dual-career families especially can be a potential problem. In this case, tell the interviewer that relocation would be considered, assuming that your spouse could continue his/her career at that locale. In fact, with the rapid increase of two-career families, many companies now offer all sorts of job placement and assistance to relocated spouses, and it would be proper to ask the interviewer if that company has any such programs.

Financial considerations, such as owning real estate here, may seem like a valid reason to you, but from a company's viewpoint, it is merely another roadblock to promotions and transfers. Wanting to be near aging or ailing parents could be acceptable for a short time, but the interviewer will want to know how you plan to handle this situation in the future. If you have still other reasons for wanting to stay in Atlanta, first try to view them from the company's perspective before you explain them to the interviewer.

In summary, you should be as flexible in your inflexibility as possible. Nevertheless, if there are legitimate reasons for your inability to more, let the interviewer know. Realize, however, that he/she may not agree that your reasons are justified for spurning their career opportunity, and so for the last time, I again suggest you carefully consider your stance on this subject. But whatever you decide, decide it *before* the interview, and be prepared with your answer.

Have questions of your own.

Either during and/or at the end of your interview, you must have several pertinent, well-conceived questions to ask. If you don't, the interviewer will think you disinterested or unintelligent; surely everything was not explained thoroughly!

There are some questions you can plan in advance to ask, but you also need to have some spontaneous questions that show you have listened and comprehended what the interviewer has said. Choose questions that show interest in the job, company and career path. Although it is important to ask questions, it is more important to ask *good* questions! And make them flow logically and spontaneously, and not sound rehearsed or "canned."

Here are some suggestions, and you will want to add more:

1) What are the projections for the growth of your company and its industry?

2) What is a reasonable career path for me to expect?

3) Why is the position open?

4) What characteristics seem to be present in your most successful employees?

5) Why has your company been so successful?

6) What problems has the company encountered in the manufacturing process [or sales, accounting, engineering, etc.]?

7) What do you want done differently by the next person to fill this job?

And here are some topics you should not discuss on your first interview, unless specifically asked:

1) Salary and benefits. Again, you should seem more interested in the job and potential with the company, than you are in immediate compensation.

2) Location, unless you can work it into the conversation without giving the impression that location is of primary importance.

3) How soon to the first promotion or salary review. Don't seem overly concerned with the next step, but rather stress how well you can accomplish the job for which you are interviewing.

Preparation is undoubtedly the most important factor in interviewing, but there are other subjects you should consider. Many of these are "givens," but let's go over them anyway.

1) **Proper dress:** Always dress conservatively and traditionally. Pay attention to details such as polished shoes, clean fingernails, limited cologne, etc. Do not wear anything distracting, such as tinted glasses or flashy jewelry. There is no excuse for failing an interview because you were inappropriately attired.

2) **Punctuality:** Always arrive a few minutes early, but never more than ten minutes. If you are not familiar with the area where the interview is to take place, make a practice trip the day or night before. As with proper dress, there is no excuse for failing the interview because you were late.

3) **Body language:** Sit up straight in the chair and do not slouch. Gesticulate some, but don't get carried away. Be appropriately animated and seem genuinely interested.

4) **First impression:** Strive to make an excellent first impression. From my own perspective and from my discussion with other interviewers, a truism to remember is that 90% of the interview occurs in the first minute! Offer a firm, dry handshake, and do not sit until told to do so. Be poised and project an air of self-confidence. Thank the interviewer for seeing you, and then wait for the interviewer to begin the session.

5) **Ending the interview:** When you sense the interview is over, again thank the interviewer for his/her time and consideration, and shake hands as you leave. If you have not already been informed of their selection process, now is the time to ask. How many additional interviews will be required, and with whom? Ask when

you can expect to hear from them, should you be selected for the position.

6) Thank you note: As soon after the interview as possible, send the interviewer a short note expressing your interest and again thanking him/her. Refer to "Chapter VI: Correspondence" for more information on this subject.

And finally a few admonitions:

1) Never chew gum and do not smoke, even if offered. If having a luncheon or dinner interview, do not drink alcohol.

2) Never use profanity.

3) Never "bad-mouth" former employers or teachers. Present a positive attitude, and avoid making any negative statements.

4) Don't make excuses for failures or mistakes. Avoid even mentioning them at all, but if you must, present them as positive learning experiences, from which you gained much insight and knowledge.

5) Be careful not to make statements that interviewers might view as "red flags." Try to imagine yourself on the other side of the desk, listening to your answers. Are you saying things that seem to disturb the interviewer? For example, I recently spoke with a former school teacher who was telling potential employers that she resigned from teaching on the advice of her psychiatrist! Almost a year later, she can't understand why she hadn't found a job!

Immediately after each interview, sit down with pen and paper, and think through the interview and your performance. Record specific questions you were asked and what a better answer from you might have been. List things you might have done better and how. What did you do well? What did you say that the interviewer seemed to like? Dislike? What have you learned from the interview that will be helpful in future interviews? This critical evaluation is extremely important; don't skip over it!

Conclusion

Interviewing--and interviewing well-- is a job in itself, and the more you do it, the better you will become. I mentioned earlier practising with a friend, and I suggest it again. Although some interviewers may not appreciate this, I also suggest that you accept one or two interviews in which you have little interest, just for the interviewing experience.

Over the past twenty years, I have interviewed thousands of applicants and overseen the interviews of countless others. In addition, I have discussed interviewing techniques with numerous corporate recruiters and compiled their thoughts also. Thus, the information I have relayed here is from personal knowledge and experience. I guarantee that if you follow my suggestions, you will have the best possible interview!

CHAPTER V

STEP FOUR:

FOLLOW-UP

CHAPTER V

Step Four: Follow-up

Pat yourself on the back; you deserve it! When you reflect on all the work you have done to get to this stage, I'm sure you feel the same.

But don't let up now! There are still a few points to cover, and these are also important in obtaining a job offer.

First of all, a thank-you note is now in order. As soon after the interview as possible, send a short note expressing your interest and thanking the interviewer(s) for his/her time. If you are sending more than one, personalize each with a comment relating to your interview with him/her. (See "Chapter VI: Correspondence" for instructions on writing this note, and to Appendix B for examples.)

Next consider this: Are there any individuals (former employers or supervisors, clients, college professors, etc.) who would attest to your abilities? If so, ask one or two of them to call the company and give you a verbal recommendation. Should that person also be regarded highly by your potential employer, this well could be the boost that takes you over the top!

The Interview Process

Most companies do not extend job offers after the first interview, unless that interview was an all-inclusive interview with several authorities. Generally, companies have a three-interview process, although this can vary widely from company to company. My personal opinion is that any company that can't make a decision within three meetings has a serious decision-making problem! However, there are companies that will drag out the interviewing and hiring process, so don't be upset if you're called for more interviews.

The first interview is a basic screening, usually conducted by a personnel representative, and this sometimes could be simply a phone interview. The second interview is most often with the primary decision-maker(s) or the person to whom the position will report. By the time you are invited back for a third interview, the decision has been made to offer you the job, or almost so. The final interviewer will be a higher authority, perhaps in corporate headquarters or at the location where you will be employed. Sometimes the second or third interview will be a simulated role playing or a sort of on-the-job situation. For example, sales applicants are frequently sent to conduct sales calls with a company sales representative; this allows the applicant to better understand the nature of the job and for the company's salesperson to relay his/her impressions of the applicant to the hiring authorities.

My reason for explaining the standard procedure is this: If you anticipate that you will be called for another interview, you must do additional research on the company before that next interview. The company will expect that if you are sincerely interested in the position, you will have done something more to learn more about them and/or their position. For example, if you are interviewing for a job in college textbook sales, you could call on a few college professors and ask about the company's books and reputation. If you are interviewing for a position as Plant Engineer, you could do research on the product they manufacture and the process involved, and have several relevant statements and questions ready to show for your efforts.

I cannot overstress the importance of this additional preparation. In practice, I have had applicants rejected after the second interview because they had not taken the time to investigate the company and position further, and thus could not display additional knowledge of the company or its products. Do this extra research; it will separate you from other applicants and impress the interviewers.

CHAPTER VI

CORRESPONDENCE

CHAPTER VI

Correspondence

Cover Letters

Think back to our discussion of resume preparation. Remember that the purpose of a resume is to get you an interview and that it must be perfect since it is to be the first impression that the company will have of you. The same is true of cover letters, and more:

1) It will be read before your resume, and thus it establishes an even earlier first impression of you than does your resume.

2) Companies realize that you may have had your resume professionally prepared, and thus the cover letter could be a more accurate reflection of you than your resume.

3) It serves as an introduction to your resume, an enticement to the reader to peruse your resume.

4) It includes information not on your resume, but requested by the company, such as salary history, restrictions and availability.

5) It can zero in on specific experience you have that fits the needs of the company.

6) It allows you to emphasize the accomplishments and achievements that illustrate your general qualifications.

It can also highlight information contained in your resume that is important and germane to the job for which you are applying. However, the purpose of the cover letter is *not* to repeat the same information in your resume. That is not necessary, since your cover letter will always be accompanied by your resume. Rather, you should emphasize factors you feel will be important to the reader and will encourage him/her to read your resume and invite you for an interview. Many examples are included in Appendix B.

Even still, that is a lot of information to include in one document! Unfortunately, the temptation to expound on every facet of your background can sometimes be overwhelming, and I have received cover letters that were even longer than the accompanying resume!

Thus, *Rule #1* in writing a cover letter is this: Keep it brief and to the point. In my discussions with other personnel managers, I find total agreement in that a short, concise cover letter is more effective than a long, detailed one. Recruiters often feel that a long, wordy letter indicates an excessively verbose person. Don't trap yourself by trying to include too much information.

Rule #2: Strive to make your cover letter appear to be a personal, original response. Your resume is somewhat generic in nature, and the cover letter is your opportunity to make it seem relevant to the company and its needs. Thus, do not adopt an obvious form letter, and never use a fill-in-the-blanks form. If you are sending out a large number of resumes and cover letters, using a word processor can be helpful in personalizing a basic form letter.

Another strong suggestion is to find out the name of the individual with whom you are corresponding, and include it on the envelope and in your letter's salutation. I realize that this is not always possible, but personnel managers really notice which applicants took the extra time to learn their name. It may seem like a minor detail to you, but some recruiters feel it is an indication of thoroughness and attention to detail.

Type your cover letter on the same paper as your resume, and proof-read it carefully for accuracy and neatness. This is the company's initial impression of you, so make it good!

Format

All cover letters have the same basic format, with some variations to suit a specific purpose. The three sections of a cover letter are Purpose, Qualifications and Closing. Usually these sections are incorporated into three paragraphs, each representing a section. Refer to Appendix B for examples.

1) *Purpose*: The Purpose section explains why you are contacting the company and for what position(s) you would like to be considered. For example, you are responding to a classified ad, you were referred by someone, or you are making a direct inquiry. One or two sentences should be enough for this.

2) *Qualifications*: Although the Qualifications section will be the longest section, it should highlight only the best of your qualifications, not explain in detail. Stress your accomplishments and achievements, and the specific experience or background that qualifies you for your job ob-jective. This section may be one or two paragraphs, depending on your layout, but it should never be more than eight or ten sentences, preferably less. You are trying to make a strong first impression by emphasizing a few hard-hitting facts. If you dilute this with a lengthy description, you will lose the impact.

3) *Closing*: End your cover letter with a standard closing paragraph of two or three sentences. First, thank the reader for his/her time and consideration. Then state your availability for an interview and indicate that you plan to call in a few days. Do not say you will call to arrange an interview. Although you want your cover letter to be aggressive and up-beat, that is too aggressive and presumptuous, and some recruiters find it offensive.

Now let's address some specific situations:

Responding to Classified Advertising

In this case, your opening Purpose sentence is simply, "I am enclosing my resume in response to your ___(date)___ classified ad for a _____."

Since you have read the ad, you have some knowledge of what the company is seeking. Thus, the objective of your Qualifications section is to show how closely you fit that job description. Refer back to the ad, and using your highlighting pen, mark the key factors sought by the company. Then tailor your letter to fit those requirements, using specific references to that ad. You may even use the same words from the ad. One very effective method is to use three or four "bullet sentences" or phrases to emphasize your qualifications that closely match their description.

In addition to the standard information in your closing paragraph, include data not in your resume but requested by the company, such as compensation or availability.

Making a Direct Contact

In the above example, you were responding to a specific opening you know existed. In making a Direct Contact, you do not have that information, and thus, your cover letter will be more open and general.

The Purpose paragraph states that you are writing to inquire about opportunities in your field or job objective. Mention why you chose to contact them (*e.g.*, you read a magazine article about them or you know of their reputation), which makes your letter seem more personal.

The Qualifications section will emphasize three to five of your career honors and/or accomplishments. Since you don't know what their needs might be, use this section to show your general patterns of achievement, and don't get too specific.

Close your letter with a standard Closing paragraph.

Referral Letters

In between the response to an ad and a blind Direct Contact letter is this situation. Here, you have been referred to the company by a source you developed through networking.

In your opening paragraph, mention the person or organization that referred you, and for what positions(s). This assumes, of course, that you have permission to use the name and that it will be known to the reader.

The content of the Qualifications section will be dictated by the amount and quality of information you were given, using a variation of the above two formats. For example, if you were told of a specific opening, use the former; if all you know is that there might be some position, use the latter.

Again, use a standard Closing paragraph.

Thank-you Notes

You may wonder if this correspondence is really necessary. Frankly, I have spoken with many interviewers who said that they attach little or no significance to these notes, and that the notes will not affect their decision. On the other hand, I have spoken with others who feel that this extra detail is indicative of a more thorough person, one who is willing to do more than may be required in order to assure success. Even those former interviewers usually admit that it could be the feather that tips the scales, when two applicants are so identically qualified. Since you have nothing to lose and much to gain by sending a short note, I recommend you do so. Several examples are included in Appendix B.

Your reasons for sending a thank-you note are

1) to thank the interviewer for his time and consideration,

2) to express your interest in the position, and

3) to reinforce the positive impression you created during your interview.

Remember this is a note, not a letter. It should be only a very few sentences, so do not go into details. Assuming you had a good interview, don't ruin it now with verbosity and overkill. If your interview did not convince the interviewer that you are a likely candidate for the position, it is too late. You should, however, re-emphasize in one or two sentences why you fit the position.

Thank-you notes can be handwritten for expediency, although typewritten is best. As always, proofread carefully for accuracy and neatness. As with cover letters, companies may feel this note is a more accurate reflection of you than your resume.

Salary History

I recently surveyed *The Atlanta Journal-Constitution* Sunday want ads, and observed that at least 90% of the professional-level, company-sponsored ads requested either a job history, current salary or salary required. In addition, numerous search firms also have begun asking that information. Some companies even stated that those resumes accompanied by salary histories would be considered first, or that resumes without a salary history would not be considered at all!

For many reasons, you often would rather not reveal your salary information prior to the interview. If your salary or salary requirements are too high or too low, you may be excluded from a job for which you are qualified and that you really want. Perhaps you are willing to accept a salary cut in order to remain in Atlanta, to gain valuable experience, to get with a more dynamic company or industry, or to change career directions. But for whatever reason, you would like not to include this requested information--but you must. How?

If you are being asked only for current salary or salary required, you can include that in your cover letter, either in the final paragraph or in a separate paragraph. If salary is not your main motivation, you can add that you are more interested in other factors than compensation. Here are some examples, and others are included in Appendix B.

> Thank you for your time and consideration, and I will call you next week to confirm that you have received my resume. My current salary is $45,000, and although I am seeking a comparable salary, I am more interested in long-range potential and opportunity with your company.

> As I am seeking to make a career change from sales into manufacturing management, I do not expect to maintain my current salary of $45,000. Rather, I am more interested in developing my new career, using my product knowledge and experience, and thus the career opportunity with your company is my priority.

However, if salary is a primary consideration, make that clear:

> Thank you for your time and consideration, and I will call you in a few days to confirm that you have received my resume. My current salary is $45,000, and I am seeking compensation in the $50,000 range.

Salary histories can be handled in one of two ways. If you have been employed for only a few years with the same company and have had no major promotions or salary increases, a simple addition to your cover letter is sufficient:

> During my five-year employment with ABC Corporation, I have progressed from a trainee salary of $23,000 to my current base

salary of $36,000. In addition, I receive a quarterly incentive bonus, up to 10% of base salary. A car and expense account are also furnished.

If you have had more than one employer or have received several promotions, you may wish to include a separate "Salary History" page. Examples are given in Appendix B.

Whether you include this information in your cover letter or on a separate sheet, keep in mind why companies want this information. The most obvious reason is to ascertain if your salary requirements are within the salary range they are offering, and there are other, more subtle reasons as well.

You may remember in our interviewing discussion that one major factor interviewers are evaluating is your life patterns--that is, demonstrated patterns of success, accomplishment, over-achievement, etc., and the opposites. If your salary history reflects a steady increase in salary, it suggests success with your company(s). If your salary has been decreasing or vacillating, that suggests problems. Also, if your salary is far below your peer group, it will be viewed negatively. Consequently, if you have some oddity in your salary history, you should explain it in one or two positively-worded sentences.

Conclusion

You may have noticed a recurrent theme running throughout this chapter--and for that matter, throughout the entire book! That theme is to keep all of your correspondence concise, to the point and relevant to your objective. Trust me on this one: company interviewers and other readers really respect the applicant who can sift out the chaff from the wheat. I am not suggesting that you exclude important information in the name of brevity, but that you learn to discern the important from the unimportant, and the most important from the less important. You need only to include the information necessary for the reader to get an accurate, positive assessment of your skills and abilities. Beyond that, you are wasting your words and the reader's time.

CHAPTER VII

CONCLUSION

CHAPTER VII

CONCLUSION

Life would indeed be nice if you received an interview from every company you contact and a job offer from every interview! Unfortunately, that is just not reality.

Dealing with rejection

In my discussions with job seekers, I have found that dealing with rejection is a very common problem. Although I am not a psychologist, I do have some observations on the matter, and I can offer some suggestions on coping with it, and even using it to your advantage.

Let's say that you contacted 25 companies, got 23 "no interests," and two interviews. (Actually that's really good! Don't be surprised if it takes _100_ calls!) The first interview was so-so, but you felt that the second interview went extremely well, and thus you are excitedly planning to do more research. Then you receive a rejection letter in the mail. Or worse yet, you never hear from them again, and they refuse to return your phone calls! How do you handle it?

All those personalized cover letters, all those phone calls, all that research---none of it paid off! But did it?

Well, for one thing, there are 25 fewer companies for you to contact! Your research taught you where to find company information, and you gained knowledge on an industry.

Most importantly, there is one more item you may be overlooking: feed-back from the interviewer. Once you know you didn't get the job, call the interviewer and very politely inquire why. Were you not qualified or did you present yourself poorly? Does he/she have any suggestions for you? Do not be argumentative, but leave with a good impression. There may be another job opening later that you will fit. If the interviewer will be honest with you, this information alone is worth all of your efforts.

But still, you must accept the fact that you will hear "No" far more often than you will "Yes." That's life, and we simply learn to expect it. During your career search, you will speak with many people---companies, agencies, network sources, *et. al.*---but unfortunately, very few will be able to assist you. Surely they would if they could, and they harbor no personal ill will toward you.

Thus, anticipate the problems and rejections you will undoubtedly encounter, and learn to face them with a positive attitude. Allot time to work on developing and maintaining your self-confidence and a strong self-image. Then begin each day with the enthusiasm needed to start over at Step One, if necessary. After all, tomorrow is another day!

Beyond rejection

If you have correctly followed the steps in the Career Search System, you should be receiving interviews and offers. If you are not, then you need to conduct some serious evaluation.

First, you should reread this book, and I'll bet you have missed some of the sources I have outlined. Have you attended any of the Job Network groups (p. 54-55)? Are you listed with the Professional Placement Network (p. 65)? Are you attending professional association meetings? Are you organized? You may even need to read this text a third or fourth time, in order to catch every suggestion mentioned.

The Career Search System includes more than enough marketing sources to obtain interviews, assuming your resume is acceptable. Have you discussed your resume with anyone? If your resume is correct and you are still not getting interviews, then you are not using all the sources at your disposal.

If your problem is getting past the interview, then I suggest you study more carefully the chapter on interviewing. Have you practiced your interview with a friend? Have you listed potential questions and your answers, and discussed them with someone who should know how to interview correctly? Do you objectively evaluate your interview after each one? Have you asked your personnel agency to critique your interview? When asking for opinions, stress you really need an honest, objective answer, and don't be overly sensitive to what you hear. Treat it as constructive criticism.

If after all this evaluation of your resume, marketing approach and interviewing ability, you are still not getting job offers, then I suggest that you may not have realistically assessed your wants or abilities, and you are interviewing for positions not available or beyond your grasp. I wish I could help you here, but that is beyond my grasp. Perhaps you should consult an industrial psychologist to gain insight into your capabilities.

The System works! I know it does, because I have seen it in action countless times. Follow it through and you will have a most successful job search.

Best wishes!

APPENDIX

APPENDIX A: SAMPLE RESUMES

The following resumes all conform to the Career Search System principles of the "Power Resume":
-- All emphasize accomplishments and achievements whenever possible.
-- They are all very positive in tone, and include no negative factors.
-- They are neat, accurate and to the point.
-- Most are one page, or two pages maximum.
-- All were typed with at least an electronic typewriter and letter-quality printer. Most were formatted using a word processor, and printed with a laser printer.

I have included examples of several different backgrounds (accountant, engineer, sales rep, etc.), formats (functional/chronological and topical) and various lay-outs. There are also resumes for a career change (named "Tanner" and "Weyrauch"), and one illustrating combining jobs ("Brooks"). In addition, you will find good examples of the use of "Objective" and/or "Summary" (or sometimes "Qualifications"), the inclusion and omission of "Personal," and various methods of describing your education.

KENNETH P. FITZPATRICK

231 E. Atlantic Street
Alpharetta, GA 30201
(404) 475-0921

Summary

Offering twenty years highly successful sales and sales management with Fortune 100 food manufacturers, frequently rating Number 1 nationally. Seeking position as **Sales Manager or Key Accounts Manager.**

Employment

Division Manager, SOUTHERN FOODS, INC. (January 1987 - present): Cover seven southeastern states selling snack foods through a ten-broker network. Call on major fast food chains and hospitality accounts, institutions and over sixty food distributors.
Added six new distributors and regained previously lost accounts. Sales increased 27% during first year and 34% during current year.

District Sales Manager, THE PILLSBURY COMPANY, Food Service Division (October 1977 - December 1986): Supervised six Sales Representatives and up to five Broker in a southeastern territory encompassing six states. Product lines included toppings chocolates, non-carbonated beverages, cheese sauces and other food products.
Was ranked #1 or #2 in percentage increase every year. Developed district into #1 district nationally for six years. Additional accomplishments available on request.

Regional Sales Manager, PROCTER & GAMBLE COMPANY, Institutional Foods Division (November 1969 - September 1977): Responsible for four Sales Representatives in three midwestern states, selling through distributors and food brokers to schools, colleges, restaurants, hospitals, etc. Products marketed included flour, bakery mixes, frozen entrees and sugar.

Sales Representataive, STANDARD BRANDS, INC., (June 1968 - October 1969): Territory sales representative, calling on retail stores in St. Louis, Missouri, and surrounding areas, selling coffee, tea, nuts, puddings, margarine, etc.

Personal

Married, three children . . . . . 5'11", 180 lbs . . . . . Open for travel and relocation . . . . . Enrolled three years at Southwest Missouri State College, studying Business Administation . . . . . Honorable discharge, U S Navy, 1965 . . . . . Hobbies include photography, bowling, water skiing and travel.

References available on request.

DAVID W. HART
1860 Ardsley Drive
Marietta, Georgia 30062
(404) 971-0316

PROFESSIONAL EXPERIENCE

Twelve years experience as a food manufacturer representative. Worked with two national manufacturers calling on grocery chains, wholesalers, and drug chain accounts, covering the states of Georgia and Florida. Attained increased sales and revenues in my market areas (i.e. 1986 vs. 1987 45% increase in sales). Extensive experience with food brokers, headquarter presentations, new item presentations, business reviews, SAMI and Nelson data, store sets, and plan-o-grams.

Responsibilities included sales and distribution for approximately 50 accounts in Georgia and Florida. Professional background has been selling food products to the grocery industry.

EMPLOYMENT HISTORY
1986 to Present

Wyeth-Ayerst Laboratories, Philadelphia, Pennsylvania
Sales Manager
Managed sales, promotions, pricing, plan-o-grams, retail accounts, and worked with SAMI and Nelson data. Full sales responsibility for grocery chains, wholesalers, and drug accounts for the sales of infant formula in Georgia and Florida. Selling and coordinating distribution with 51 major accounts with total sales of $6.7 million in 1987. Performed under an MBO system for bonuses and pay raises.
Accomplishments:
•45% sales increase - 1986 vs. 1987
•42 new item placements in 1987
•Managed Eckerd Drug Company account
•Managed major food brokerage companies in Georgia and Florida

1985 to 1986

Russell Communications, Atlanta, Georgia
Sales Representative
Worked in a privately owned company calling on business owners to sell communication systems. Built up clientele by referrals and cold calling.

1974 to 1984

Sunshine Biscuit Company, Atlanta, Georgia
Account Manager
Supervised and coordinated activities of two major retail accounts. Full sales responsibility, which included promotions, business reviews, credits and new item presentations. Also maintained 55 other retail accounts.
Accomplishments:
•30% sales increase per year for three consecutive years with Kroger account
•1976 received Salesman of the Year Award for the highest sales

EDUCATION

B.B.A. Georgia State University, Atlanta, Georgia

111

WENDY C. BLOOM

Temporary address:
348 Bulldog Drive
Athens, GA 30601
(404) 353-7621

Permanent address:
1234 Azelea Rd NW
Atlanta, GA 30327
(404) 262-7890

Summary

Recent college graduate majoring in International Business and Spanish. Career objective is employment with a multi-national corporation, preferable with operations in Latin America. Areas of interest include marketing, international banking and finance, and import/export operations.

Education

UNIVERSITY OF GEORGIA, Bachelor of Business Administration, graduation planned for June, 1989. Relevant curriculum has included the following:

Macro and Micro Economics	Statistics
Principles of Accounting I & II	Commercial Spanish
International Marketing	Business Law I & II

Employment

IBM Corporation (Summer Internship, 1988): Diverse duties giving exposure to the operations of a major multi-national corporation. Worked in both Marketing and Personnel departments, under minimal supervision. Operated IBM 5520 Word Processor.

Elson's Gift Shops, Atlanta International Airport (Summers 1985 - 1987):
Sales Clerk, using Spanish and Portuguese languages daily in serving international passengers.

U S Army Hospital, Fort Benning, GA (Summer 1984): Medical Clerk, working with wounded Salvadoran military personnel.

Personal

Born January 23, 1966 . . . . . Single, excellent health . . . . . Open for travel and relocation, including international . . . . . Fluent in Spanish and Portuguese . . . . . Interests include international events, reading and art.

References available on request.

112

CHARLES G. PULLER

244 Mecklenburg Ave
Greeensboro, NC 28664
(919) 954-1042

Objective

To secure a position in Manufacturing Management, either in production, operations or administration, where education, abilities and experience can be best utilized.

Experience

JOHN H. HARLAND COMPANY, printer of bank stationery and other commercial printing. (1981 - Present)

PRODUCTION MANAGER, Greensboro, NC (1986 - present):
Have profit center responsibility for subsidiary involved in technical printing (forms, stationery, cards and mail order checks) and related direct mail operations. Direct the activities of four Supervisors managing a staff of 40 persons. Oversee inventory/quality control, efficiency, personnel, audit preparation and purchasing. Extensive involvement in overall company efficiency planning.

> *Accomplishments*: Reduced labor costs by 5% per month. Boosted profit margin by 4% (from minus 2% to plus 2% level). Won "Best Quality Division" awards (1987 and 1988). Reduced turnover from over 50% to under 20%.

ASSISTANT PLANT MANAGER, Orlando, FL (1983 - 1986):
Supervised staff of 15 administrative employees in a check printing facility. Directed all daily operations in such areas as personnel management, accounting, safety, audit preparation, billing, customer service, purchasing, security, attitude surveys, customer relations and P&L statements. Served as Sales/Plant Coordinator for 13 Sales Representatives in Colorado, Wyoming, Utah and Montana.

> *Accomplishments*: Heavily involved in planning and implementation of move into new printing facility. Received three "A's" on periodic plant audits. Developed new Employee Training Manual later utilized in three plants. Established procedure that reduced weekly billing errors by over 40%.

PLANT SUPERINTENDENT, Orlando, FL (1981 - 1983):
Directed activities of 50 production employees and five supervisors in a check printing facility. Managed production planning, scheduling, maintenance, quality control, inventory control and cost containment.

> *Accomplishments*: Increased operational efficiency by 12% per year. Improved delivery time from 79% to 93%. Established quality standards for employees, reducing rerun rate from 3.4% to 2.6%.

Education

MASTER OF BUSINESS ADMINISTRATION, concentration in accounting, University of Florida, 1989. GPA 3.8/4.0.

BACHELOR OF SCIENCE in Industrial Management, North Carolina State University, 1980. GPA 3.7/4.0.

References available on request.

C. David Holbrook
4002 Walnut Court
Rolling Meadows, Illinois 60008
(312) 397-7412

Objective

Senior manufacturing/engineering management position

Summary

Seven years senior management experience in manufacturing extending from factory operations to multi-facility responsibilities. Achievement in factory modernizations, tightly timed new product introductions and significant capacity increases. Expertise in cost reduction, quality improvement, materials control, employee relations and strategic planning. Results oriented. MBA from the University of Chicago.

Experience

Schwinn Bicycle Company, Chicago, Illinois, since 1986

Director of Manufacturing
Responsible for all domestic manufacturing for this leading bicycle manufacturer with plants in Wisconsin and Mississippi. Management responsibilities include: materials requirements planning (MRP), capacity planning, staffing and industrial relations, quality assurance (QA), facility maintenance, automation planning, and cost management. Manage a staff of 200 through four direct reports and a budget of approximately $19 million. Report to the chief financial officer.

Results:
- Assessed existing staff, reorganized where necessary and upgraded the professional factory staff.

- Upgraded the manufacturing process, virtually eliminating frame alignment defects, saving $228,000 annually.

- Doubled on time delivery performance while increasing production volume by 45%.

- Developed a program to use temporary labor to off set cyclical market demands, saving the company $150,000 in labor costs.

- Managed the successful implementation of the manufacturing process for an all new state-of-the-art aluminum bike; the first entirely new (non-steel) bike in Schwinn's history.

- Installed cost control system enabling the organization to better measure factory expenses.

Wilson Sporting Goods Company sb1P (formerly a division of PepsiCo, Inc.), River Grove, Illinois, 1980-1986

Director of Engineering Services
Managed a professional staff of 28 through four direct reports. Responsible for process automation, facilities engineering, industrial engineering and operations planning in 13 domestic and foreign factories and four distribution centers. Reported to the senior vice president, operations.

114

Experience   **Results:**
(continued)   ■   Established a manufacturing cost reduction program which saved over $21 million
                            during a five year period (approximately 3% of the annual manufacturing costs).

                        ■   Accomplished a critical $3.7 million tennis ball capacity expansion in concert with
                            the introduction of a blow molded tennis ball "can" and a new specialty product.

                        ■   Built a composite tennis racket factory in Kingstown, St. Vincent and transferred
                            the manufacturing equipment from the U.S. in time to meet demanding production
                            requirements.

                        ■   Responsible for $1.7 million of new process equipment and facilities which
                            produced two new golf ball products against a tightly timed introductory schedule.

                        Procter & Gamble Company, Cincinnati, Ohio and Jackson, Tennessee, 1961-
                        1980

                        Engineering Manager, Jackson facility, 1978-1980

                        Results:
                        ■   Provided design services for automated cookie mix production.

                        ■   Accomplished energy conservation projects which reduced utility costs by 11%.

                        Operations Manager, Jackson facility, 1974-1977
                        Managed 250 production and technical personnel manufacturing Pringle's Potato Chips
                        (annual sales of $36 million).

                        Results:
                        ■   Improved productivity 24% through a series of projects which reduced staff 33%
                            and headcount by 20%.

                        ■   Produced three consecutive test market products on schedule and under budget.

                        Chemical/Industrial Engineering Manager - Jackson facility, 1970-1973
                        Operations Manager - Cincinnati facility, 1968-1969
                        Prepared Mix Packaging Department Manager - Cincinnati, 1965-1967
                        Prepared Mix Industrial Engineer - Cincinnati, 1964
                        Deodorizer Department Manager - Cincinnati, 1961-1963

Military   United States Navy, Lieutenant, Destroyer Moale, 1958-1961

Education   M.B.A, Executive Program, University of Chicago, 1985
                        B.I.E, Georgia Institute of Technology, 1958

                        Honors: Tau Beta Pi - Engineering Honor Society
                                        Alpha Pi Mu - Industrial Engineering Honor Society

Personal   Born October 21, 1936; Married, three children; Height 6'; Weight 185; Health excellent.

MICHAEL J. BROOKS, C.P.A.

1988 Powers Ferry Road
Smyrna, GA 30339
(404) 432-4789

Objective

Auditing and/or Accounting Management

PRIVATE ACCOUNTING EXPERIENCE
November 1984 - present

Combination of employment and consulting primarily in the health care field, both in manufacturing/distribution and service industry. Have supervised five personnel in handling all corporate financial reporting, including journal entries, account analysis, payroll (250 employees), accounts payable/receivable, budgeting and financial analysis. Successfully automated manual system to computer-based. Working knowledge of Medicare and Medicaid procedures.

PUBLIC ACCOUNTING EXPERIENCE
June 1981 - October 1984

As Senior Accountant, ran various audits for clients, from preliminary stage through drafting of financial statements. Completed corporate, partnership and individual tax returns. Clients were mostly in commercial construction, health care and food service. Instructor on Lotus software and supervised two staff accountants.

Education

BACHELOR OF SCIENCE in Accounting, University of Florida, 1981.
Activities: Elected Student Government Senator, played Varsity Football one year, and was member of fraternity. Earned 80% of college tuition and expenses as part-time warehouse laborer.

Data processing knowledge and experience includes Lotus and Symphony software, and IBM PC, IBM System 38 and Tandem mainframe.

Personal

Born April 14, 1957 . . . . . 5'10", 170 lbs . . . . . Married, two children . . . . . Open for travel and relocation . . . . . Active in civic affairs, especially United Way and High Museum of Art . . . . . Interests include all sports, golf and contemporary art.

References available on request.

MARK W. TANNER
5547 Roswell Road NE, Apt. S-5
Atlanta, GA 30342
(404) 843-5678

Objective

To apply experience gained in management, physical therapy and training to a corporate environment. Open for travel and relocation.

Experience

Management: More than seven years supervisory experience of up to ten employees. Interview and hire office and support staff. Handle accounting and bookkeeping functions, client liaison and sales/marketing strategies.

Training: Train all clerical and administrative employees. Write and develop training programs for individual and client needs. Conduct lectures, seminars and platform training classes for up to fifty persons, including managers and other trainers. Highly skilled in one-on-one patient care and education.

General: Past employment has all involved extensive public contact and has required exceptional communicative skills, oral and written, on a variety of levels. Have developed excellent research skills.

Employment

Operations Manager, Goodhealth Fitness Center, Inc. (1982 - present): Hire, train and supervise office and professional staff for Physical Therapy facility, which combines the benefits of medical expertise with an exercise center. Responsible for clinical aspects of patient care, education, class development, and progress evaluation. Also handle communications with physicians and other consulting professionals.

Prior employment has been as **Physical Therapist** for two major health centers, Dekalb General Hospital and Sinecure Holistic Health Center, conducting both in-patient and out-patient treatment.

Education

BACHELOR OF SCIENCE in Biology, University of South Carolina, 1975. Graduated Phi Beta Kappa.

Certificate in Physical Therapy, University of Oklahoma, 1974.

Additional graduate-level courses taken at Georgia State University and Southern Technical Institute in Physical Therapy and Technical Writing.

References available on request.

SHAUN H. McDONOUGH

3580 Northside Drive NW
Atlanta, GA 30305
(404) 231-9988

Objective

Seeking career in Insurance and Risk Management. Long range career plans include training in several facets of the insurance industry, including Underwriting, Claims Adjusting, Loss Prevention, Risk Management and other related fields. Immediate employment objective is a trainee position with a major insurance company.

Education

BACHELOR OF BUSINESS ADMINISTRATION in Risk Management and Insurance, University of Georgia, graduation planned for December, 1989. Will graduate in the top 10% of the Business School.

Honors/activities: Dean's List several times, GPA 3.4/4.0, elected to membership in Beta Gamma Sigma (business honor society), recipient of academic scholarship for excellence in insurance curriculum, member of Insurance Society.

Experience

Several years of retail sales in family-owned clothing store during high school and college. Worked full time during first year of college and during summers. Also assisted with formal bookkeeping functions, including general ledger entries, accounts payable and receivable, payroll and financial statements.

Most recently have been employed part-time at local distribution warehouse, in a shipping and receiving position.

Personal

Born November 17, 1965 . . . . . Married, no children . . . . . 5'10", 165 lbs, excellent health . . . . . Open for travel and relocation . . . . . Interests and hobbies include physical fitness, reading and personal investments.

References available on request.

LOUIS C. CARTWELL

1234 Apple Lane NW
Atlanta, GA 30342
(404) 250-0215

Summary

MBA graduate with five years management experience in United States Army as commissioned officer. Seeking Management Development Program with a major corporation, utilizing well-developed supervisory skills.

Experience

UNITED STATES ARMY
(June 1984 - present)

CAPTAIN, eligible for promotion. Available for employment October 1990. Summary of duties and responsibilities follows:

Maintenance Management: As Company Maintenance Officer, coordinated all scheduled and unscheduled maintenance for organic vehicles, engineer and support equipment from 1985 to date. Managed training of all maintenance personnel and equipment operators to insure cost effective utilization of manpower and material.

General Management: Managed safety program for the 8th Aviation Company in 1986 - 1987. As Safety Officer, identified areas of high accident potential, suggested corrective actions and educated unit personnel in accident proofing techniques. Managed Unit Postal Facility serving eighty men. While Platoon Leader in an aviation unit, motivated and trained up to 25 men in the accomplishment of a wide variety of activities. Served six months as Financial Custodian over funds for 1,000 dependent children,

Aviation: Received private pilot's license in 1984. Completed Army Aviation helicopter training with honors in 1985 and received FAA commercial helicopter certification. Have flown 850 accident-free hours to date flying VIP missions in support of the Division Commanding General and his staff.

Education

MASTER OF SCIENCE in Business Administration with honors, Boston University, 1987. Completed program while working full-time in the Army.

BACHELOR OF BUSINESS ADMINISTRATION in Management, North Georgia College, 1984. Served as President, Student Government Association. Active in Sigma Nu fraternity, distinguished Military Graduate.

Personal

Born November 27, 1963. . . . . 6'0", 170 lbs, excellent health. . . . . Married, one child. . . . . Open for travel and relocation. . . . . Interests include historical reading, tennis, racquetball and physical fitness. . . . . References available on request.

SUSAN LYNN WEYRAUCH
5034 Odin's Way
Marietta, Georgia 30067
(404) 992-0482

A results-oriented manager, with more than seven years of achievement in training, development and administration.

OBJECTIVE
A management position in training and development or in sales and marketing.

EDUCATION
BOSTON COLLEGE, Chestnut Hill, Massachusetts, 1978
BACHELOR OF ARTS, Education, MAGNA CUM LAUDE
Dean's List, all semesters
Most Valuable Player, Water Polo, Fall, 1976. Varsity Letter in Swimming.

PROFESSIONAL ABILITIES
TRAINING
- Received special recognition for superior technical training of co-workers in specialized instruction strategies.
- Trained and supervised over 150 workers in basic skills competencies, providing effective corrective ar positive feedback.
- Documented detailed policies and procedures to enhance delivery of organizational objectives.
- Effectively analyzed causes of worker performance problems; recommended, implemented and monitore the alternatives.
- Conducted ongoing performance appraisals at regular intervals.
- Motivated and coached workers to improve productivity and to achieve successful performance.

PROGRAM DESIGN
- Organized, developed, implemented courseware and systems for work management, basics instruction ar training development.
- Analyzed job tasks, established measurable objectives, tracked performance and successful completion assignments.
- Created successful performance feedback systems and established system to monitor and record results
- Planned and produced audio-visual coursewares.
- Developed and administered pre and post evaluations of job performance.
- Organized, planned and conducted educational tours, related to increasing job knowledge ar performance.

COMMUNICATION SKILLS
- Vast multi-cultural experiences have developed the ability to relate to people of all walks of life.
- Developed and delivered presentations to groups of up to 100 people.
- Counseled, interviewed and negotiated with co-workers, management, public officials and the general publ to enhance inter-communication and working relationships.
- Edited reports, researched, composed and distributed written information and materials.

EMPLOYMENT HISTORY
1979 to 1985	Educator	Okinawa, Jap
	Department of Defense Dependent Schools	Stuttgart, West Germa
1978 to 1979	Educator, East Cobb Middle School	Marietta, Georg

ADDITIONAL INFORMATION
Worked and traveled extensively in the Far East and Europe for more than six years. Proficient in French a German. Will relocate and travel.

120

Gary Alexander
231 South Street
Anderson, California 99999
(111) 555-0101

EXPERIENCE

Acme Chemicals, Anderson, California Phone: (111) 555-2000

Process Engineer—January 1986-Present

Responsible for directing and controlling a number of distinct chemical processes including blends and specialty chemicals for the plastics, automotive, and textile industries.

Achievements:
- Implemented a quality program that allows the middle 30% of a product's specifications to be obtained consistently.
- Implemented a statistical process control program on 25 products that have improved quality 15%, prevented off quality, and increased production associates' awareness and involvement in preventing off quality.
- Aided in research and development of 5 new fiber finish products. Prepared pilot plant and production process procedures. Drafted standards for all products which include machine and labor cycles.
- Aided in the design and start-up of a $400,000 capacity expansion for a polyolefin clarifier.
- Implemented a cost reduction program for a polyolefin clarifier which cut total variable conversion costs by 9.6% for $75,000 annual savings with zero capital investment. Presented results of cost reduction breakthroughs at corporate sharing rally to the President and C.E.O. of Acme and Company.
- Have completed 400 hours of continuing education in such areas as public speaking; computer training in Autocad, Lotus, and Wordperfect; Statistics; Managerial Grid; Organic Chemistry; and CPR.

Dependable Environmental Services, Inc., Atlanta, Georgia (404) 555-0000

Field Analytical Technician—Summers of 1984 and 1985

Responsible for observation, documentation and all sampling techniques on asbestos abatement projects; including project leader on major asbestos abatement projects in Memphis, Tenn. and Charleston, South Carolina.

EDUCATION BACKGROUND

Bachelor of Science, **Chemical Engineering.** December 1985
Georgia Institute of Technology, Atlanta, Georgia.
Earned 50% of education expenses.

Honor Graduate, Secondary School. June 1981
St. Boniface Academy, Scarsdale, New York

COLLEGE ACTIVITIES/HONORS

- American Institute of Chemical Engineers (A.I.C.H.E.), GT Chapter, 1983-85
- Elected Board Member of Student Center, 1982-85
- Homecoming Committee, 1983-84
- Alpha Sigma Delta Phi Honor Society, 1981-82

References available upon request

GILMORE S. ALLEN
789 Marilyn Drive
Decatur, GA 30020
(404) 292-9876

OBJECTIVE	Marketing or sales position with a product- or service-oriented firm where experience and qualifications can be effectively used. Seeking career opportunity conducive to personal and professional growth.
QUALIFICATIONS	**Background and Scope of Development:** Currently employed as Marketing Representative with Xerox Corporation. Prior experience with IBM Corporation and First Atlanta Bank. Master's Degree and Bachelor's Degree in Business Administration. **Capabilities:** Three years of corporate sales experience has involved such areas as cold calls, prospecting, territory management and extensive sales training.
EXPERIENCE	**XEROX CORPORATION** June 1984 – Present **Marketing Representative** - Market entire office product line of computers, typewriters, copiers, facsimile and systems. Activities include developing new accounts and managing established accounts. Achievements: Consistently surpass sales performance goals. **IBM CORPORATION** February 1983 – May 1984 **Marketing Support Intern** - Responsibilities included cold calls, selling and training IBM equipment for the general sales force. Accomplishments: Achieved highest sales ranking of the year during internship. **FIRST ATLANTA BANK** September 1980 – January 1983 **Financial and Budget Analyst** - Prepared detailed financial data including the assets and liabilities of First Atlanta Bank and holding companies, and presented monthly to senior management.
EDUCATION	Samford University, Birmingham, AL **MASTER OF BUSINESS ADMINISTRATION,** June 1983 **BACHELOR OF SCIENCE,** June 1980 **Activities:** Served as President of Alpha Kappa Psi, business fraternity; Vice-President, Pi Kappa Phi, social fraternity; President, InterFraternal Council.

APPENDIX B: CORRESPONDENCE

All job-related correspondence should conform to these two rules:

(1) Keep it brief, relevant and to the point.

(2) Make it as personal as possible.

The following cover letters and thank-you notes illustrate those principles. In addition, observe that they are very positive in tone, with an emphasis on achievements, when possible.

Finally, remember your purpose in writing these correspondences:

-- Including a cover letter with your resume is to create a good, strong first impression and thus get your resume read.

-- If you include a separate salary history page, your purpose is not only to relay information requested, but also to continue on the positive track created through your cover letter and resume.

-- A thank-you note should express your interest in the position and reinforce the positive impression you made during your interview.

Keeping these objectives in mind will help you compose your documents.

(Cover Letter Sample 1)

1234 Pineland Drive NW
Atlanta, GA 30327
September 28, 1989

Procter & Gamble Distributing Company
7890 Tide Road
Butler, GA 30345

Dear Sirs:

In response to your recent advertisement for a distribution management position, I am enclosing my resume. As you will see from my experiences, I am an over-achiever with a demonstrated pattern of success.

In addition to my B.B.A. in Operations Management, which I entirely self-financed, I have five years of distribution-related experience in the areas that you specified in your ad. As a First Lieutenant in the US Army, I supervised more than forty persons in the operation of a Distribution Center, including shipping/receiving, warehousing, inventory control and material management. I received outstanding evaluations and Officer Efficiency Reports.

Thank you for your time and consideration, and I look forward to hearing from you soon. I am available for interviews immediately.

Sincerely yours,

Joseph B. Caan
(404) 255-3456

(Cover Letter Sample 2)

876 Sprayberry Lane
Charlotte, NC 28241
November 17, 1989

Mr. John Adams
Human Resources Manager
Union Camp Corporation
4341 Paper Bag Lane
Savannah, GA 31404

Dear Mr. Adams:

I am enclosing my resume and salary history in response to your recent advertisement for a Marketing Development Manager. I am additionally familiar with Union Camp through Bill Smith, one of your Sales Managers in Savannah, and a former business associate. We worked together on a quality control problem at our company's Miami facility, and he has offered to be one of my references.

I have eight years of highly successful sales and promotion experience in the wood products industry. I have exceeded my weekly sales quotas by 40%, resulting in a total sales increase of 18%. I attribute this success to my strong problem-solving and interpersonal skills, and my ability to develop a close and creditable relationship with my customers.

Thank you for your time and consideration, and I will call you in a few days to confirm that you have received my resume. I am available for an interview at your convenience.

Sincerely yours,

Steve Jarvis
(704) 237-8724

(Cover Letter Sample 3)

1594 Arden Rd NW
Atlanta, GA 30327
August 8, 1989

Ms. Deborah Teagle
ABC Software Development Company
100 Peachtree St NE
Suite 2104
Atlanta, GA 30303

Dear Ms. Teagle:

I am a college graduate in Computer Management and have two years programming experience. I am writing to you to inquire if you have present or projected needs in my field, and I have enclosed my resume for your perusal.

During my two years with XYZ Corporation, I have been rated a "5," which is the highest evaluation possible.

Thank you for your time and consideration. I would appreciate the opportunity to meet with you at your earliest convenience and look forward to hearing from you soon.

Sincerely,

Anna K. DeHoff
(404) 264-8631

(Cover Letter Sample 4)

879 Ridge Point Drive
Smyrna, GA 30339
April 7, 1989

Mr. John Thompson, Director of Personnel
Chicken Little Company
456 Corn Street
College Park, GA 30365

Dear Mr. Thompson:
Thank you for your time on the phone today and for the information regarding your current need for an Industrial Engineer. As you requested, I am enclosing my resume for your review.

During my three years with ABC Textiles, I have been responsible for implementing and managing projects very similar to the ones you described to me. A few of my recent assignments include these:
-- Organized and conducted a study to determine and document causes of dye department downtime.
-- Designed, estimated cost and proposed layout for relocation of maintenance shop, resulting in a 20% increase in efficiency.
-- Assisted Safety Department in training employees on the proper use of new machinery, resulting in a decrease of 25% in time lost due to accidents.

Thank you again, and I look forward to hearing from you soon. My current salary is $37,000 annually, and I am available for relocation.

Sincerely yours,

Lynn K. Parsons
(404) 433-4898

4011 Roswell Rd NE, #F-6
Atlanta, GA 30342
November 18, 1989

Cartwell Chemical Company
7890 Riviera Parkway
Jacksonville, FL 32306

Dear Sirs:

Under my direction, production planning has been optimized at multiple facilities, including contract manufacturers and overseas facilities.

As you are advertising for an experienced Department Manager, you may be interested in my qualifications:
-- As Inventory Control Manager, I reduced inventories from $50M to $42M, while improving product availability.
-- I designed and implemented a material recovery program that saved more than $175,000 annually.
-- Working with the MIS Department, I installed a new computerized database and operating program, substantially reducing inventory loss.

In addition, I have a Master's degree in management and a Bachelor's degree in chemistry.

Thank you for your time and consideration. I will call you soon to confirm that you have received my resume. I am available for interviews at your convenience.

Sincerely yours,

Celia Mosier
(404) 250-1234

(Cover Letter Sample 6)

4488 Springdale Lane
Asheville, NC 28766
January 22, 1989

Mr. Calvin Reynolds, Region Sales Manager
ABC Laboratories, Inc.
3333 Interstate Parkway
Marietta, GA 30367

Dear Mr. Reynolds:

I am contacting you at the suggestion of Mike Douglas, the ABC Laboratories Sales Representative who handles our account. I am seeking to make a career change, out of purchasing and into a medical sales position. My resume is enclosed for your perusal.

My five years of experience as a hospital purchasing agent has given me valuable insight into the problems encountered by both your sales force and their clients, and I believe that knowledge will be most helpful in my new career. In addition, I have recently received my Bachelor's degree in marketing, while employed full-time at Grady Hospital.

I realize that my current salary of $32,000 may be higher than the salary generally offered to entry-level sales representatives, and thus I am flexible in my compensation requirements. My primary concern now is to establish a career in medical sales.

I trust my experience and initiative will be desirable attributes for ABC Laboratories, and I will call you next week to answer any questions you may have. I am available for an interview at your convenience.

Sincerely yours,

John G. Taylor
(704) 896-3748

MARVIN B. DAVIS

3345 Peachtree Road NE
Atlanta, GA 30326
(404) 262-7331

SALARY HISTORY

Bruce D. Morgan & Associates, Importers (1981 - Present):

National Sales Manager (1986 - present)
$47,500 salary + commission + bonus

Region Sales Manager (1983 - 1986)
$35,000 salary + commission

Sales Representative (1981 - 1983)
$18,000 salary + commission

All positions included company car and expense account.

Seeking initial compensation of $50,000. Long range advancement and income incentives are paramount. Will consider lower salary/draw with high commission potential.

Edmond R. Smith

1200 Franklin Road NE, Apt. F-1
Atlanta, GA 30342
(404) 847-1234

Salary History

Western Union Telegraph Company (December 1981 - present)

Senior Internal Auditor (4/88 - present)	$ 41,150
Supervisor Financial Control (4/85 - 4/88)	39,600
Regional Staff Manager (11/84 - 4/85)	37,150
Internal Audit Supervisor (12/81 - 11/84)	32,300

E. L. Lowie & Company (November 1978 - November 1981)

Assistant Controller	$26,500

Convenient Systems, Inc. (September 1976 - November 1978)

Divisional Controller (8/77 - 11/78)	$21,000
Accounting Manager (9/76 - 8/77)	15,600

A. M. Pullen & Company (June 1972 - September 1976) $13,500

LURLINE C. HARRIS

231 E. Rock Springs Rd NE
Atlanta, GA 30324
(404) 876-2388

SALARY HISTORY

Hillside Energy and Automation (March 1987 - present)

Director of Compensation and Benefits $55,000

Citizens and Southern National Bank (May 1984 - March 1987)
Senior Compensation Analyst $47,000
Compensation Analyst   42,000
Exempt Recruiter   35,000

(Note: Income reduction accepted in order to enter
corporate Human Resources.)

Blinders Personnel Service (July 1981 - May 1984)

Accounting Division Manager $49,000
Senior Recruiter   40,000
Staff Recruiter   18,000

(Thank-you Note Sample 1)

231 E. Rock Springs Rd NE
Atlanta, GA 30324
November 18, 1989

Mr. Thomas C. Browder
Hillside Energy and Automation
235 Peachtree St NE
Suite 2330
Atlanta, GA 30303

Dear Mr. Browder,

Thank you and your staff for the time you spent with me today. I very much enjoyed learning more about Hillside Energy and Automation and the new compensation program you are developing. With my five years of compensation and benefits experience, I am certain I can give excellent direction to your program and would greatly enjoy the challenge.

I look forward to hearing from you soon.

Sincerely yours,

Lurline C. Harris
(404) 876-2388

(Thank-you Note Sample 2)

789 Spring St. NE, #F-8
Marietta, GA 30067
June 21, 1989

Mr. John C. Mentor
First Atlanta Bank
2 Peachtree St NE
Suite 1234
Atlanta, GA 30303

Dear Mr. Mentor,

As a recent college graduate, I realize that although my business experience is indeed limited, my potential is vast! My achievements and accomplishments to date illustrate the pattern of success I am certain I will continue.

Thank you for your interview time today at the University of Georgia's Career Day. I am very interested in First Atlanta's Management Development Program, and I feel that I have much to contribute. I look forward to hearing from you soon.

Sincerely yours,

Wendy C. Bloom
(404) 874-8394

(Thank-you Note Sample 3)

789 Park Drive NW
Snellville, GA 30098
September 8, 1989

Mr. Charles J. Lamb
Mobil Chemical Company
P O Box 78
Covington, GA 30302

Dear Mr. Lamb,

Thank you for your time and information yesterday, and especially for the tour of your facility. With your state-of-the-art equipment, I can easily understand why Mobil Chemical has been so successful, and I would like the opportunity to contribute to that success.

As I stated during our interview, I have been the top sales representative in my district with Scott Paper Company for the past three years. That achievement illustrates the abilities I also could bring to Mobil.

Thank you for your consideration. I am available for further interviews at your convenience.

Sincerely yours,

Jim Gibson
(404) 928-5673

APPENDIX C: SELECTED COMPANIES

The following employers are among the largest hiring companies in Atlanta. These companies were selected primarily based on the large number of "professional-level" employees hired annually, but also for diversity and variety. In developing a direct contact marketing strategy, these are the ones you should contact on your own. Smaller companies that hire only a few employees each year are not a good source to direct contact, unless you have specific experience in their industry. The CAREER SEARCH SYSTEM includes other sources to reach those smaller companies.

I believe that I have included here at least 90% of the Atlanta companies that hire 25+ "professional-level" employees each year, but if you encounter one that I omitted, please let me know. One exception to this, however, is that there are certain industries (*e.g.*, fast foods) and specialties (*e.g.*, RN's) for which there are nearly infinite needs. I have not tried to include all of those hiring companies, but rather a few of the largest.

EXPLANATION OF TERMINOLOGY

This book is primarily for "professional-level" individuals, usually with a college degree (although not always or necessarily), and thus the positions I am describing are of that level. I have frequently made use of the terms "exempt" and "non-exempt" in describing positions, and unless you have worked in a personnel department, you may not be familiar with their meaning. These terms relate to the federal wage and salary laws, and without boring you with a lengthy explanation of a complex system, just remember that generally speaking, most on-going career positions with executive potential are called "exempt" (that is, they are exempt from the federal wage and salary laws), although there are numerous exceptions. For example, banks frequently hire individuals into non-exempt Teller positions, and then promote into exempt positions when one occurs. Other companies like to hire recent college grads in non-exempt positions, in order to learn their business "from the bottom up."

This explanation may seem irrelevant to you now, but since it does affect your time and income, I have noted it in my company descriptions. Also knowing the number of exempt employees at a specific company will give you a general ideal of the career potential there.

Another term you may not understand is "MIS," the abbreviation for Management Information Systems, and which has become the generally accepted acronym for data processing and computer positions.

DISCLAIMER

The information contained herein was obtained from company officials and/or published sources, and is believed to be accurate. However, the author and publisher assume no liability for errors or the consequences thereof. Employment figures are generally approximate and can fluctuate. I would greatly appreciate information regarding any errors or omissions, and comments about any companies contained here. Send any information to P O Box 52291, Atlanta, GA 30355.

CONTINUOUS UPDATES

As you know, *Atlanta Jobs* is totally revised and updated annually. In addition, we are constantly updating all materials, including this company list--adding, deleting and revising when changes occur. As an additional service, Career Publications will mail you this updated information. Send $3 to cover postage, handling and printing to

CAREER PUBLICATIONS
56 E. Andrews Dr NE, Suite 29, Atlanta, GA 30305.

These updates will be mailed out as quickly as each order is received.

SELECTED COMPANIES

Note: See preceding page for explanation of terms used.

A T & T
Since court-ordered divestiture of the gigantic Bell System, AT&T has undergone tremendous consolidation and reorganization. AT&T has more than 18,000 employees in Atlanta, working in many different offices and branches throughout the city, and that number is expected is increase. Many of these offices conduct their own recruitment, and by far, the largest of these is AT&T Company. In addition, AT&T Network Systems also does significant hiring. Thus, the following three personnel departments are listed:

A T & T Company
Profile: Southern Region Headquarters for long distance services, covering a 14-state territory. All exempt hiring is handled through this office, and they have needs for both recent grads and experienced personnel in sales and sales support; engineering (mostly EE and ME); MIS; and MBA. Fewer needs for liberal arts majors than other more specific degrees. Has co-op programs and internships in engineering, marketing and computer science, and The Inroads Program for minorities.
Procedure: Send resume to Management Employment,
1200 Peachtree St NE, 100 Colony Square, Room 660, Atlanta, GA 30309.
(404) 888-3681

A T & T Network Cable Systems
Profile: Manufacturing facility producing communications cable--wire, copper and fiber optics. Employs 3400, including 1000+ exempt. Hires recent grads in accounting/finance, engineering (all types, especially EE, ME and ChE) and MIS, and experienced personnel in sales only.
Procedure: Accounting/finance and sales, send resume to Personnel; engineering and MIS, send resume to Technical and Professional Dept. Both at 2000 Northeast Expressway, Norcross, GA 30071.
(404) 447-2000

A T & T Network Systems
Profile: Southern Region Headquarters location, with over 2000 employees here. Hires many "Engineering Technical Associates," who are primarily two-year engineering grads. Four year grads hired are mostly EE and sales representatives.
Procedure: Send resume to Personnel Department,
6701 Roswell Rd NE, Atlanta, GA 30328.

(404) 573-6228

ALLSTATE INSURANCE
Profile: Provides support for the sales staff of this property and casualty insurance company. This office employs 250, with approximately 60% exempt. Will hire up to 50 recent grads each year: accounting/finance majors (including MBA's), economics majors and other business degrees. Likes liberal arts majors for claims trainees. Also hires sales trainees and underwriting trainees. Hires few experienced exempt, as most positions are filled by promotions.

Procedure: Send resume to Human Resources,
Suite 600, 5500 Interstate North Pkwy, Atlanta, GA 30328.
(404) 953-7253

AMERICAN CANCER SOCIETY
Profile: One of the largest non-profit health organizations in the US, ACS moved its corporate headquarters from New York to Atlanta in 1988. Employs 325 in headquarters (150 exempt), plus local and state offices here. Rarely hires recent grads, but will need experienced personnel in accounting/finance, management and other specialized areas (*e.g.*, Public Relations Reps, creative services and writers for publications, A-V specialists for film production, etc.).

Procedure: Send resume to Personnel,
1599 Clifton Rd NE, Atlanta, GA 30329.
(404) 320-3333

AMERICAN RED CROSS
Profile: Non-profit emergency assistance and blood bank, employing 500 in Atlanta, including 125 exempt. Does campus recruiting for accounting/finance, nurses, medical technologists and lab technicians. Also seeks about 20 new social studies grads each year for community relations positions in donor resources. Experienced personnel are needed in the same areas, plus MIS (HP 3000 and IBM 36).

Procedure: Send resume to Director of Personnel,
1925 Monroe Drive NE, Atlanta, GA 30324.
(404) 881-9800

AMERICAN SOFTWARE, INC.
Profile: Atlanta-based corporation that develops, manufactures and markets software for business applications. Employs 650, most of whom are exempt, and they are expecting an increase in total employment. Rarely hires recent grads, but will hire 100+ experienced exempt, nearly all in MIS (IBM 38), including programmer analysts and systems analysts, or sales-related. MIS applicants must have 2+ years experience in software

140

development using IBM hardware; sales applicants should have 5+ years software sales experience.

Procedure: Send resume to Manager of Corporate Recruiting,
470 East Paces Ferry Rd NE, Atlanta, GA 30305.
(404) 261-4381

AMOCO FABRICS & FIBERS CO.-- Research & Development Center

Profile: R&D and information services center for manufacturer of high tech fabrics, fibers and yarns used in industrial, commercial and residential applications (mostly carpets). Employs 165 in R&D and 25 in info services, with 50% exempt; expects an increase in employment. Hires no recent grads, but seeks many engineers (ChE and textiles mostly) and chemists-- BS, MS and PhD level--plus MIS (IBM).

Procedure: Send resume to Human Resources Representative,
P O Box 43288, Atlanta, GA 30336.
(404) 941-1711

ARROW CO.

Profile: Manufactures Arrow-brand clothing. Employs 1000 total, with 125 exempt, and expecting an increase. Seeks 10+ recent grads each year, mostly for production management, engineering (IE, IET mostly) and MIS (IBM). Experienced needs in same areas, plus accounting.

Procedure: Send resume to Industrial Relations,
3725 Zip Industrial Blvd, Atlanta, GA 30354.
(404) 761-2808

ANDERSEN, ARTHUR & CO.

Profile: "Big 6" Certified Public Accounting firm, and largest CPA firm in Atlanta. Has three divisions--accounting, tax and management information consulting-- and employs 1100 total, including 600+ accountants. Hires 200 recent grads each year for the three divisions, and seeks accounting/finance, computer science majors, and MBA or MAcc degrees. Hires very few experienced accountants, and they must enter the same training program as recent grads.

Procedure: Send resume to Director of Recruiting,
133 Peachtree St NE, 25th floor, Atlanta, GA   30303.
(404) 658-1776

ARBY'S, INC.

Profile: Corporate headquarters for the ninth largest restaurant chain in the world. Employs 220 in corporate office with about 75 exempt. Corporate rarely hires recent grads, but will hire 30 experienced personnel, mostly in accounting/finance, marketing, food technology, real estate and MIS (IBM 38). Has need for 100 restaurant managers (recent grads and experienced), who are hired through the region office.

Procedure: For corporate headquarters positions, send resume to Employment Coordinator,
3495 Piedmont Rd NE, Suite 700, Atlanta, GA 30305.
For management positions, contact Regional Manager,
8300 Dunwoody Place, Suite 201, Dunwoody, GA 30338.
(404) 587-3246

ARTHRITIS FOUNDATION
Profile: Corporate headquarters for this non-profit organization, providing education and fundraising activities relative to arthritis disease. Employs 130 with 40% exempt, and expects a slight increase. Hires only a few recent grads (accounts, MIS and journalists) and will hire 30 experienced exempt as accountants, MIS (DEC VAX), fundraisers, program coordinators, writers and other editorial staff.
Procedure: Send resume to Employment Coordinator,
1314 Spring St NW, Atlanta, GA 30309.
(404) 872-7100

THE ATHLETE'S FOOT
Profile: Corporate headquarters for this specialty retailer in athletic footwear. Has 460 stores nationwide, including 165 company-owned (others franchised). Employs 160 at headquarters, and is expecting an increase. Most recent grads hired are for Retail Management Training or an occasional accountant. Hires 30 experienced personnel in accounting/finance, MIS (IBM), retail operations, buyers and franchise coordinators.
Procedure: Send resume to Personnel Manager,
3735 Atlanta Industrial Pkwy, Atlanta, GA 30331.
(404) 696-3400

ATLANTA GAS LIGHT COMPANY
Profile: Public gas utility headquartered in Atlanta. Employs 1200 with 250 exempt. Hires only recent college grads, mainly engineers (ME, CE, IE) and accountants.
Procedure: Send resume to Personnel Department,
P O Box 4569, Atlanta, GA 30302.
(404) 584-4712

ATLANTA JOURNAL-CONSTITUTION
Profile: Largest newspaper in the Southeast, employing 5900 (many of whom are part-time) with 600 exempt. Hires 200 recent grads per year, in all areas. However, recent journalism grads need some work experience with a smaller newspaper. Also will hire up to 150 experienced personnel, again in all areas and including journalists. In addition, they offer 50 internships each year in journalism, advertising and business.

Procedure: For employment as a journalist, reporter or intern in the newsroom, send resume to Managing Editor; other applicants, send resume to Employment Manager.
72 Marietta St NW, Atlanta, GA 30303
(404) 526-5151

ATLANTA LIFE INSURANCE CO.
Profile: Corporate headquarters for the largest black stock-owned insurance company in the US, founded in 1905. Markets group health and life insurance in 13 states, and employs 165 at headquarters. Hires only a few recent grads on an as-needed basis in accounting/finance, MIS and actuarial. Hires experienced personnel in accounting/finance, sales and MIS.
Procedure: Send resume to Assistant VP, Director of Personnel,
100 Auburn Ave NE, P O Box 897, Atlanta, GA 30301.
(404) 659-2100

BBDO/ATLANTA
Profile: Largest advertising agency in Atlanta, headquartered in NYC. Employs 150 with approximately 110 exempt. Hires a few recent grads, mostly for lower-level positions, but with good opportunity for advancement. Offers internships in media and creative departments. Hires experienced advertising personnel and accountants.
Procedure: Accountants should send resume to CFO; advertising professionals, send resume to CEO. Both at
3414 Peachtree Rd NE, Suite 1600, Atlanta, GA 30326.
(404) 231-1700

BANKSOUTH
Profile: Corporate headquarters for the fourth largest bank in Georgia (assets) and has 64 branches. Employs 2100 total, including 500 officer-level. Recent grads are hired in accounting and auditing, or for "Management Associate Program" (hired throughout the year). Experienced exempt needs are banking professionals, accounting/finance, and MIS (IBM 38). Will hire up to 200 new employees each year in all functions.
Procedure: Send resume to Human Resources Division,
Mail Code 8, P O Box 5092, Atlanta, GA 30302.
(404) 529-4111; non-exempt Job Hot Line: 529-4285

BELLSOUTH
BellSouth is the largest corporation headquartered in Atlanta and the Southeast, generating revenues of $13.7B in 1988. BellSouth employs 100,000+ in seven southeastern states, and with 20,000+ of those located here, it is also one of Atlanta's three largest corporate employers.

All BellSouth subsidiaries fall into two categories, "regulated" (i.e., regulated by various statutes) and "non-regulated." The regulated companies employ 17,000 of the total here, in three primary subsidiaries:

1) BellSouth Corporation -- This is the holding company for all BellSouth companies.

2) BellSouth Services -- Provides all centralized staff support functions for the two operating telephone companies, Southern Bell and South Central Bell.

3) Southern Bell -- The operating telephone company serving areas of GA, SC, NC and FL.

Nearly all other BellSouth Subsidiaries are non-regulated.

In 1989, the Georgia regulated companies consolidated their numerous employment offices into two:

1) BellSouth Management Employment Center, which handles exempt employment

2) Southern Bell General Employment Office, which hires mostly non-exempt.

Each non-regulated BellSouth company continues to conduct its own hiring, and I have included here the most active of those.

BellSouth Advertising and Publishing Corp.

Profile: Responsible for sales and information included in BellSouth Yellow Pages. Employs approximately 1100, with 50% exempt. Hires recent grads and experienced personnel in sales (40+ annually) and graphic arts.

Procedure: Send resume to Employment Manager,
2295 Park Lake Dr, Suite 490, Atlanta, GA 30345.
(404) 491-1900; Job Information Line: 491-1747

BellSouth Enterprises

Profile: Holding company for non-regulated BellSouth subsidiaries. They conduct hiring for smaller subsidiaries, as well as their own corporate staff. Most needs are for accounting/finance backgrounds--some recent grads, but mostly experienced, and certification is highly desirable.

Procedure: Send resume to Employment Manager,
1201 Peachtree St NE, Suite 803, Atlanta, GA 30309.
(404) 249-4000

BellSouth Management Employment Center

Profile: Conducts all exempt employment for BellSouth's regulated companies. Has needs for nearly every conceivable job description, and will hire up to 400 each year for Atlanta. Also hires 50 summer interns and co-op students in all areas.

Procedure: Send resume and cover letter to
P O Box 54300, Atlanta, GA 30308-0300
(404) 249-2000; 249-2779 Job Line, gives current needs.

BellSouth Mobility

Profile: Headquarters for wire-line provider of cellular communications service in 24 SE cities. Employs 450+ in Atlanta (1/2 exempt), and will have an increase, mostly in other SE cities. Hires 10 recent grads and 100 experienced exempt each year in accounting/finance, sales, engineering (EE and radio engineering), and MIS (IBM with MSA software). Has needs for MBA's in finance and marketing, and has product development section.

Procedure: Send resume to Director of Personnel,
5600 Glenridge Dr NE, Suite 600, Atlanta, GA 30342.
(404) 847-3600

Southern Bell General Employment Office

Profile: Hires non-exempt employment for Southern Bell/Georgia's regulated companies. Most needs are for marketing graduates to be in customer service/telemarketing (hired 150 in 1989) and for two- and four-year technical graduates to be technicians (hired 100 in 1989).

Procedure: Do not send resume. Write or call for application to be mailed to you, or stop by their offices and get one.
2835 Brandywine Rd, Suite 408, Chamblee, GA 30341
(404) 452-5110

BIG B DRUGS

Profile: Atlanta district office of Birmingham-based Bruno's Corp., conducting the hiring of store managers and pharmacists for 71 metro-Atlanta stores. Hires recent grads and experienced exempt, and expects to hire 200 in 1990.

Procedure: Send resume to Personnel Supervisor,
515 Wharton Circle SW, Atlanta, GA 30378.
(404) 699-9351

BIG STAR SUPERMARKETS

Profile: Division of Grand Union Company, based in New Jersey. Second largest food chain in Southeast, with 58 stores in Atlanta employing 5500 total. Hires 20 recent grads and up to 100 experienced personnel, almost entirely for store management. All accounting/finance and MIS at corporate headquarters.

Procedure: Send resume to Vice President of Personnel,
P O Box 105525, Atlanta, GA 30348.
(404) 765-8300

BLUE CROSS/BLUE SHIELD OF GEORGIA

Profile: BC/BS is the nation's largest health care insurer, although each member company operates autonomously. This office employs 700 with 200 exempt. Recent grads with no related experience are usually hired into non-exempt positions, then promoted when an exempt position occurs; many are hired annually into accounting and insurance specialties. Experienced exempt are needed in accounting/finance, sales, management and insurance specialties (risk management, underwriting, etc.) No engineering needs and few MIS.

3350 Peachtree Rd NE, Atlanta, GA 30326.
(404) 842-8000

BULL HN INFORMATION SYSTEMS, INC.

Profile: Formerly Honeywell-Bull, Inc., still owned by Honeywell, Inc. of the US, Groupe Bull of France and NEC Electronics of Japan. Manufactures and sells computers. Employs 300 in Atlanta, plus this office is the South Central Operations Center and handles all hiring for 22 states and Puerto Rico. Seldom hires recent grads, and most hires are experienced sales, sales management and technical support personnel with computer experience.

Procedure: Send resume to Senior Staffing Specialist,
6 West Druid Hills Dr NE, Atlanta, GA 30329.
(404) 982-2000

BYERS ENGINEERING CO.

Profile: Atlanta-based company that provides engineering and computer graphic services for major telephone operating companies. Two divisions, each conducting their own recruitment: Information Systems hires only experienced MIS (DEC VAX); engineering division requires telephony experience.

Procedure: Send resume to Human Resources Manager at the appropriate division; both located at
3285 Barfield Rd, Atlanta, GA 30328.
(404) 843-1003 x402 for information systems; x320 for engineering

CABLE NEWS NETWORK (CNN)

(See Turner Broadcasting System)

CENTERS FOR DISEASE CONTROL

Profile: Atlanta-based federal agency, responsible for research and control of disease. Employs 3000 in Atlanta, and hires several hundred laboratory and medical research specialists annually, recent grads and experienced. Engineers hired are environmental, ME, IE and safety. Hires a few accountants and MIS (IBM), and seeks many liberal arts graduates and BBA's for "Public Health Associates."

Procedure: Send resume to Chief, Recruitment and Placement
1600 Clifton Rd NE, Atlanta, GA 30333.
(404) 639-3656; 639-3615 Job Information Line

CHICK-FIL-A, INC.

Profile: Corporate headquarters for 400-unit fast food chain. Chick-fil-A does not own or franchise units; rather, each unit is individually owned and operated, and thus they do not hire for restaurant management. Headquarters

146

staff numbers 175+, and an increase is expected. There will be openings for entry-level accountants, and for experienced exempt in marketing, legal and operations management assistance.

Procedure: Send resume to Personnel Supervisor,
5200 Buffington Rd, Atlanta, GA 30349.
(404) 765-8127

CHROMATICS, INC.
Profile: Atlanta-based manufacturer of high performance color graphic work stations, employing 500. Most needs are for engineers (EE generally). Seldom has opening for MIS or accounting.

Procedure: Send resume to Director of Personnel,
2558 Mountain Industrial Blvd, Tucker, GA 30084.
(404) 493-7000

CIBA VISION CARE
Profile: Division headquarters for Ciba-Geigy unit that manufactures, distributes and conducts research/development of soft contact lens and eye care products. Total employment in Atlanta is 1450, with 600 exempt. Currently hires few recent grads. Seeks experienced exempt in numerous specialties, including manufacturing managers, product managers, accountants, sales reps, R&D Scientists (polymers, micro-biologists, etc.) and MIS personnel (AS 400).

Procedure: Send resume to Staffing Specialist,
2910 Amwieler Ct, Atlanta, GA 30360.
(404) 448-1200

CITIZENS AND SOUTHERN NATIONAL BANK (C & S)
Profile: Largest bank in Georgia and subsidiary of the newly proposed Avantor Financial Corp., to be the second largest southeastern bank holding company, corporate headquartered in Atlanta and Norfolk, VA. Employs 5000+, with about 30% exempt. Hires 75 recent grads each year, mostly accounting/finance, management and MBA's. Hires 150 experienced personnel (mostly with financial services backgrounds) in accounting/finance, management and MIS (IBM).

Procedure: Recent grads, send resume to Manager of College Relations; experienced personnel, send resume to Management Recruiting. Both at
P O Box 4899, Atlanta, GA 30302-4899.
Job Information recordings: (404) 897-3578 for recent grads, 897-3021 for experienced personnel; general information at 897-3357.

THE COCA-COLA COMPANIES
Coca-Cola and Coca-Cola Enterprises are the first and third largest Fortune 500 corporations headquartered in Atlanta. There are several autonomous hiring groups, as listed below:

Atlanta Coca-Cola Bottling Co.

Profile: Bottles and distributes Coca-Cola brands of soft drinks, and a division of Coca-Cola Enterprises. Employs 1500+, including 275 exempt. Hires both experienced personnel and recent grads into sales, accounting, engineering and manufacturing operations.

Procedure: Send resume to Personnel,
100 Galleria Pkwy NW, Suite 700, Atlanta, GA 30339.
(404) 951-7000

Coca-Cola USA

Profile: Corporate headquarters and flagship operating unit for sales and distribution of Coca-Cola and allied brands. This is the primary hiring unit of Coke, and they will hire more than 50 exempt personnel for Atlanta only (many more for other locations) in accounting/finance, laboratory positions, marketing, advertising and a few engineers.

Procedure: Send resume and cover letter to Employment Manager,
P O Drawer 1734, Atlanta, GA 30301.
(404) 676-3898

Coca-Cola Corporate

Profile: Provides staff support for Coca-Cola subsidiaries world-wide. Employs 1400, with 950 exempt, and there will be a slight increase in data processing personnel in the future. Hires no entry-level, only experienced personnel, mostly in finance-related areas. Also hires some for their legal department and in research and development.

Procedure: Send resume to Corporate Staffing,
P O Drawer 1734, Atlanta, GA 30301.
(404) 676-3701

Coca-Cola Enterprises

Profile: Support headquarters for bottling operations of Coca-Cola brands of soft drinks. Each bottling company operates automously (see listing for Coca-Cola Bottling Co.), and thus this office employs only 250. Hires only experienced personnel, mostly in accounting and finance, and will have a slight increase.

Procedure: Send resume to Employment Manager,
P O Box 1778, Atlanta, GA 30301.
(404) 676-6279

COHN & WOLFE/ATLANTA

Profile: Corporate headquarters for the largest Public Relations firm in Atlanta and the 17th largest in US. Expects an increase in employment. Most personnel hired are experienced P R professionals. Only recent grads hired are those with internship experience or extensive writing experience, especially with campus news publications. Offers internships during spring and summer quarters for PR majors in their junior and senior years at college.

Procedure: Send resume to Operations Manager,
              225 Peachtree St NE, Suite 2300, Atlanta, GA 30303.
              (404) 688-5900

CONTEL CORP.
Profile: Telecommunications service provider, with corporate headquarters in At-
              lanta. This office employs 1400, with 60% exempt, and conducts hiring
              for many Contel subsidiaries, including Contel Cellular. Anticipates
              hiring 20 recent grads and 200 experienced exempt personnel each year, in
              accounting/finance, human resources, marketing (no sales), engineering
              (EE mostly) and MIS (IBM and DEC).
Procedure: Send resume to Manager of Professional Staffing,
              P O Box 468356, Atlanta, GA 30346.
              (404) 395-8716

CONTEL CUSTOMER SUPPORT
Profile: National headquarters location for Contel subsidiary that sells, installs and
              services telecommunications equipment. Employs 75 here, plus this of-
              fice handles staffing needs nationwide. Seldom hires recent grads, but
              seeks experienced exempt in accounting, engineering (EE mostly), pur-
              chasing, human resources and other central office support types. No
              MIS.
Procedure: Send resume to Manager, Human Resources,
              1117 Perimeter Center West, Suite W-200, Atlanta, GA 30338.
              (404) 698-5800

COTTON STATES INSURANCE GROUP
Profile: Atlanta-based property and casualty insurance company, with 430 total
              employees and 200 exempt. Hires a few recent grads in insurance-related
              fields, especially risk management and actuarial. Will also hire 30+
              experienced personnel, mostly in accounting, property and casualty
              claims, underwriting, human resources and MIS.
Procedure: Send resume to Employment Manager,
              P O Box 105303, Atlanta, GA 30348.
              (404) 391-8600

COURTYARD BY MARRIOTT
Profile: Region headquarters for this moderate-priced, mid-size hotel chain de-
              signed to attract business persons and family vacationers, not large con-
              ventions. Growing rapidly and expects an increase in total employment.
              Will hire many recent grads into hotel management (related degree not
              necessary) and sales training, and experienced personnel in hotel man-
              agement.
Procedure: Send resume to Human Resources Manager--Recruitment,
              380 Interstate North Pkwy, Suite 400, Atlanta, GA 30339.

(404) 955-6608

CRAWFORD & CO.
Profile: Provides insurance industry and risk management industry with full spectrum of services, primarily claims-related. Corporate headquarters in Atlanta employs 800, and they have branches throughout the US. Hires 100+ recent grads each year, mostly in casualty claims adjusting (BBA best, but others ok). Has summer internship program in Risk Management. Experienced personnel are hired for accounting/finance, MIS, risk control and health and rehabilitation.
Procedure: For claims adjustors (including trainees); risk control; and health and rehabilitation personnel, send resume to Personnel Manager,
SE Region Office, 5780 Peachtree Dunwoody Rd, Atlanta, GA 30342.
(404) 256-0830
Accountants and MIS personnel, send resume to Personnel, P O Box 5047, Atlanta, GA 30302.
(404) 847-4080

DAYS INNS OF AMERICA
Profile: Atlanta-based hotel/motel chain, third largest in the world. Owns or manages 25+ units and has 900+ franchised, plus 475 under development. Corporate office employs 550 total, with 200 exempt. Recent college grads are hired on an as-needed basis, probably ten per year, mostly in accounting/finance. Experienced accounting/finance and MIS are needed (operates two IBM 3090's), plus occasional needs for MBA's. In addition, some hotel sales and management personnel are hired through this office (probably 10 recent grads and 40 experienced personnel), although not necessarily for Atlanta.
Procedure: Send resume to Manager, General Employment,
2851 Buford Hwy NE, Atlanta, GA 30324.
(404) 728-4276

DECATUR FEDERAL S&L
Profile: Corporate headquarters for third largest Savings and Loan in Georgia. Employs 900 total, 250 exempt, and anticipating a slight increase in total employment. Hires 25 recent grads each year, mostly in entry-level banking or accounting/finance. Some new hires may be non-exempt initially, to be promoted into an exempt position when one becomes available--they have an in-house job posting system.
Procedure: Send resume to Personnel Department,
250 East Ponce de Leon Ave, Decatur, GA 30030.
(404) 371-4372

DELOITTE & TOUCHE

Profile: Third largest CPA firm in Atlanta, newly created in 1989 with the merger of two of the former "Big 8" international CPA firms, now referred to as the "Big Six." Has accounting/audit, tax, small business (called "middle market") and consulting divisions. Consulting division hires recent MBA's with strong accounting, and experienced exempt with specific industry experience; will hire 20 in 1990. Other three divisions will hire approximately 60 each year. (Note: The merger may alter some of this information.)

Procedure: For Consulting Division, send resume to Consulting Recruiting Manager; for other three divisions, send resume to Recruiting Coordinator. Both at
100 Peachtree St NE, Suite 1800, Atlanta, GA 30303.
(404) 220-1500

DELTA AIRLINES, INC.

Profile: Headquartered in Atlanta and the largest airline serving Atlanta, Delta employs 21,000 here and is one of Atlanta's three largest corporate employers. Only experienced personnel hired are for pilots, flight attendants and reservation agents. Otherwise, a career path with Delta means starting in an hourly position, such as baggage handler, mechanic or clerk, and working up.

Procedure: Obtain an application form, complete it and return that plus your resume to Employment Office, listed below. Application firms are available by calling their office, but the easiest method is to go by any Delta ticket office, including the airport, and request one.
P O Box 20530, Hartsfield International Airport, Atlanta, GA 30320
(404) 765-2501

DIGITAL COMMUNICATIONS ASSOCIATES

Profile: Corporate headquarters location that designs, manufactures, services and markets data network communications products. Employs 1500 with 600+ exempt, and they expect an increase in employment. They will hire 20+ recent grads and 100+ experienced personnel each year, mostly electrical engineers, computer science majors and marketing. DCA utilizes DEC equipment and is an IBM vendor.

Procedure: Send resume to Employment Manager,
1000 Alderman Drive, Alpharetta, GA 30201.
(404) 442-4000

DIGITAL EQUIPMENT CORP.

Profile: World's second largest manufacturer of computer systems, with 1600 employees in Atlanta and expecting an increase. Hires liberal arts and technical recent grads, as well as experienced personnel, into all disciplines-- sales, engineering, MIS, accounting/finance, marketing analysis, management, etc.

Procedure: Send resume to Employment,

5555 Windward Pkwy West, Alpharetta, GA 30201-7407
(404) 772-2955

DOBBS INTERNATIONAL
Profile: Provides airline catering service at Atlanta airport. Employs 1300 in At-
             lanta, 20% exempt. Will hire 25+ exempt annually (experienced and
             trainee), mostly for production management positions. Operates fleet of
             85 trucks, and thus has needs for transportation specialists.
Procedure: Send resume to Manager of Personnel Services,
             P O Box 45485, Atlanta, GA 30320.
             (404) 530-6300

EASTERN AIRLINES
Profile: 1989 was an interesting year for EAL, and I have not been able to contact
             anyone who can give definite employment projections for 1990.
Procedure: Past procedure was to obtain an application in the main terminal of the
             Atlanta airport and mail to Employment Office--ATLLK, Hartsfield
             International Airport, Atlanta, GA 30020.
             (404) 762-2195 - generic recording

ECKERD DRUGS
Profile: Operates 95 retail stores in Atlanta, employing 1400 total with 350 ex-
             empt. This office hires almost entirely for store management, and will
             hire for Atlanta positions 100 recent grads as trainees ("Assistant Store
             Manager") and 50 experienced retail managers.
Procedure: Send resume to Human Resources Mgr--Atlanta Region,
             36 Herring Rd, Newnan, GA 30265.
             (404) 688-8770

ELECTROLUX CORP.
Profile: Corporate headquarters for international manufacturer and distributor of
             vacuum cleaners and other home cleaning products and services. Employs
             250+ at headquarters, with 30% exempt. Hires some recent grads, but
             prefers experience, for accounting/finance, administration and MIS (IBM).
             Sales reps are hired by local sales offices.
Procedure: Send resume to Human Resources Representative,
             2300 Windy Ridge Pkwy, Suite 900 South, Marietta, GA 30067.
             (404) 933-1000

ELECTROMAGNETIC SCIENCES, INC.
Profile: Atlanta-based company that designs, manufactures and sells microwave
             components, microwave sub-systems and radio-link terminals. Employs
             650+, with 225 exempt, and expects an increase. Hires a few recent grads
             in accounting and engineering (mostly ME and EE), and hires 30+

152

experienced personnel in all areas--accounting/finance, sales, engineering and MIS (DEC). Has six co-ops in engineering.

Procedure: Send resume to Personnel,
125 Technology Park, Norcross, GA 30092.
(404) 448-5770

EMORY UNIVERSITY/EMORY UNIVERSITY HOSPITAL

Profile: Private, Methodist-affiliated university with 9000 students. Employs 5000 non-faculty, and anticipates a slight increase in total employment. Only recent grads hired would be in scientific research or for non-exempt positions, awaiting an exempt opening. Will need 50+ experienced personnel in accounting/finance, administration, engineering, MIS (IBM) and research. Prior academic experience is not required for most positions. Hospital has 600+ beds and is also a teaching and research institute. Hospital hires recent grads in medical specialties, such as nursing, pharmacology, respiratory/physical therapy, etc.

Procedure: For hospital and university positions, send resume to Emory University Personnel Department,
637 Asbury Circle, Atlanta, GA 30322.
(404) 727-7611

ERNST & YOUNG

Profile: Nation's largest CPA firm, formed in 1989 with the merger of two "Big 8" CPA firms. Employs 700 in Atlanta, with 550+ exempt. Has three divisions: consulting, audit and tax. Consulting group's strengths are in health care, information systems and corporate/finance services, and seeks applicants with 3+ yrs business experience (financial, marketing or operations management), and preferably with MBA. Other divisions seek mostly recent accounting and MBA grads.

Procedure: For consulting division, send resume to Manager of Recruiting--Consulting, at 2100 Gas Light Tower, 235 Peachtree St NE, Atlanta, GA 30303.
For audit positions, send resume to Director of Human Resources; for tax positions, send resume to Director of Tax Recruiting. Both at 1800 South Tower, 225 Peachtree St NE, Atlanta, GA 30303.
(404) 581-1300 - Common switchboard for all three divisions.

EQUIFAX, INC.

Headquartered in Atlanta, Equifax is one of the nation's two largest credit and information gathering companies. There are eight subsidiaries, employing 2500 total in Atlanta, and the three largest hiring units are listed below.

Equifax, Inc.--Corporate Headquarters

Profile: Headquarters staff totals 800 with 250 exempt. Will hire 50+ (recent grads and experienced) each year in accounting/finance and computer science. Insurance background helpful.

Procedure: Send resume to Personnel Manager,
              P O Box 4081, Atlanta, GA 30302.
              (404) 885-8000

Equifax Services
Profile: Largest business unit of Equifax, serves primarily the insurance industry, providing underwriting and claims information. Most hiring (50/yr) is for MIS (IBM and DEC), experienced and trainee. Also seeks marketing grads for research and analysis positions, and liberal arts grads for customer service and field representatives. Insurance background helpful.
Procedure: Send resume to Division Head--Employment,
              2 Midtown Plaza, 1360 Peachtree St NE, Suite 1100, Atlanta, GA 30302.
              (404) 870-2500

Credit Bureau, Inc.
Profile: Second largest Equifax subsidiary, and is an on-line data base providing consumer and commercial credit reports, collections and credit card promotions to the credit granting industry. Growing at 25% annually and will have 10% increase in employment. Hires both recent grads and experienced exempt in accounting/finance, branch operations management and MIS. Also seeks recent MBA's in accounting/finance and experienced MBA's in marketing.
Procedure: Send resume to Technical Employment Representative,
              P O Box 4091, Atlanta, GA 30302.
              (404) 885-8400

EQUITABLE REAL ESTATE INVESTMENT MANAGEMENT, INC.
Profile: National headquarters in Atlanta. One of 70 subsidiaries of the giant Equitable Insurance Company, and one of the most profitable. Manages $33 billion in real estate assets throughout the US and Japan. Employs 300 total at headquarters, most of whom are exempt. Only recent grads hired are for accounting/finance, probably 5+ per year. Will hire 50+ experienced exempt, some in accounting/finance, but mostly in MIS; converting from IBM/Wang to all IBM 3090. Also has orientation program for MBA's, preferably from top school, and with 2+ years experience in financial or real estate environment.
Procedure: Send resume to Director of Human Resources,
              3414 Peachtree Rd NE, Atlanta, GA 30326-1162.
              (404) 239-5000

FEDERAL HOME LOAN BANK OF ATLANTA
Profile: One of four regional offices that acts as the credit reserve bank and the regulatory agency that supervises the Savings and Loan industry. Since the passage of the S&L bailout legislation, this federal agency is going through many changes, which will be completed by the end of 1990. This office will continue to hire for both themselves and the newly cre-

ated Office of Thrift Supervision. Employs over 600 total in Atlanta, more than half of whom are exempt, and they anticipate an increase to more than 1000 in 1990. Will hire 50+ recent grads in accounting/finance and MBA's, and 100+ experienced personnel in accounting/finance, MIS and MBA's. Backgrounds in banking or with another regulatory agency is ideal.

Procedure: Send resume to Manager of Employment,
1475 Peachtree St NE, Atlanta, GA 30309.
(404) 888-8000

FEDERAL RESERVE BANK OF ATLANTA
Profile: Head office for the Sixth District of the Federal Reserve System. Oversees the functions of five southeastern Federal Reserve Banks, makes recommendations regarding monetary policy to the Federal Reserve Board, and serves as the "banker's bank" for member banks in the Southeast. Employs 900, with 400 exempt. Will hire up to 15 recent grads in accounting/finance, MIS and MBA's. Will hire 60± experienced personnel in accounting/finance, data-base analysis, department management and MIS (IBM-oriented). Commercial banking experience preferred.

Procedure: Send resume to Employment Specialist,
104 Marietta St NW, Atlanta, GA 30303-2713.
(404) 521-8326

FIRST AMERICAN BANK
Profile: Atlanta's sixth largest bank, formed in November 1987, when First American Banks of Washington, D.C. purchased National Bank of Georgia. Management training program is called "First Advantage" and starts in February and July. There will be openings for trainees and experienced personnel, in accounting and operations management, as well as for banking professionals.

Procedure: Send resume to Human Resources Department,
2000 RiverEdge Parkway, Atlanta, GA 30328.
(404) 951-4016 for information; 951-4010 Job Line, including directions to their employment offices.

FIRST ATLANTA BANK
Profile: Third largest bank in Georgia and subsidiary of First Wachovia, headquartered in Winston-Salem, NC. Employs 5300 total in Georgia, with 2400 exempt. Will hire 50 recent grads each year, for all areas of the bank, and their management training class begins in June. Probably 100 experienced exempt personnel will be hired annually, again in all areas of the bank, and including those with banking experience. Some MIS (IBM) needed, although most is in NC.

Procedure: Send resume to Human Resources,
2 Peachtree St NW, Suite 1234, Atlanta, GA 30303.

(404) 332-5000

FIRST FINANCIAL MANAGEMENT CO.
Profile: Atlanta-based information services company, offering a broad range of data processing and related services through diverse customer base. Employs 350, approximately one-third exempt. Hires mostly MIS personnel (Unisys system), probably 50 each year, either experienced or recent grad with computer science major (tech school grads OK, too). Also seeks a few accounting/finance personnel, recent grad and experienced, and sales representatives with banking backgrounds. (See also Georgia Federal Bank and Microbilt subsidiaries.)
Procedure: Send resume to Personnel Manager,
3 Corporate Square, Suite 700, Atlanta, GA 30329.
(404) 321-0120

FIRST UNION NATIONAL BANK OF GEORGIA
Profile: Fifth largest bank in Georgia, and subsidiary of First Union Bank, headquartered in Charlotte, NC, one of the largest bank holding companies in the Southeast. Operates 60+ branches in the Atlanta area, employing 1300, including 350+ exempt personnel. Expects to hire 25 trainees, mostly through campus recruiting during November through May, for classes beginning in January, May and September. Will also hire 75 experienced personnel, including accountants and banking professionals.
Procedure: Send resume to VP and Manager of Personnel,
55 Park Place, GPP Pers 17, Atlanta, GA 30303.
(404) 827-7135

FORD MOTOR COMPANY
Profile: This facility assembles Ford Taurus and Mercury Sable cars, employing 2800 hourly, 285 salaried and 250 professional personnel. Most exempt hiring for this facility is for electrical engineers (trainee and experienced) in manufacturing management, plus some needs in industrial relations (MBA best). Accounting/finance is centralized in Detroit.
Procedure: Send resume to Salaried Personnel Office,
340 Henry Ford II Avenue, Hapeville, GA 30354.
(404) 669-1546

FOOTE & DAVIES
Profile: Largest commercial printer in the southeast, printing mostly mail-order catalogues and magazines. Employs 560 with 120 exempt. Recent grads are hired for accounting and cost estimating positions, and experienced personnel are needed as printing salesmen and customer service account executives.
Procedure: Send resume to Personnel Manager,
3101 McCall Drive NE, Atlanta, GA 30340.

(404) 451-4511

FULTON FEDERAL SAVINGS BANK
Profile: Georgia's oldest and second largest Savings and Loan institution, head-quartered in Atlanta, and employing 600 with 20% exempt. Hires recent grads for accounting and auditing positions, as well as entry-level management trainee positions. Has limited management training program, but hires non-exempt "Teller Trainees" to go into management as needs arise. Seeks experienced banking professionals, auditors and accountants.
Procedure: Send resume to Human Resources,
600 West Peachtree St NW, Atlanta, GA 30308.
(404) 249-7346

FUQUA INDUSTRIES
Profile: Corporate headquarters for this Fortune 500 corporation. Very small support staff here (total 45 employees), and thus does minimal hiring. All subsidiaries conduct their own hiring. (see Snapper Power Equipment.)

GEC AVIONICS
Profile: Corporate headquarters for the US subsidiary of GEC Avionics Ltd. of England. Electronics manufacturer, whose major products include "Heads-Up" display for fighter aircraft, as well as CO_2 laser range finders. Employs 280 with 50% exempt. Rarely hires recent grads, but will hire up to 50 experienced personnel, mostly in electrical engineering and physics. Also hires MIS and an occasional accountant.
Procedure: Send resume to Personnel Manager,
P O Box 81999, Atlanta, GA 30366.
(404) 448-1947

GENERAL ELECTRIC COMPUTER SERVICES
Profile: National headquarters for GE subsidiary that does maintenance, leasing and repair of industrial, electrical and test instruments, and compute equipment. Most recent grads hired are in engineering and MIS (DEC and Prime) or for technician positions. Hires experienced personnel in accounting/finance, sales and MIS.
Procedure: Send resume to Staff Consultant,
6875 Jimmy Carter Blvd, Suite 3200, Norcross, GA 30071.
(404) 843-6200

GENERAL MOTORS

Profile: GM has had two large assembly facilities in Atlanta, but will be closing
            one in 1990. The remaining facility (CPC Doraville) anticipates a de-
            crease in employment, and will have no exempt needs.

GEORGIA FEDERAL BANK
Profile: Corporate headquarters for Georgia's largest S&L, purchased in 1989 by
            First Financial Management Company. (See separate listing.) Employs
            1300 total. Hires a few recent grads for management training program,
            and they also seek experienced accounting/finance and professional
            bankers.
Procedure: Send resume to Recruiting,
            241 Peachtree St, Atlanta, GA 30303.
            (404) 330-2400

GEORGIA INSTITUTE OF TECHNOLOGY
Profile: Third largest university in Georgia and second largest in Atlanta, with
            12,000+ students. Has 3500 employees (including faculty), with
            approximately 500 exempt. Technical and engineering employees are
            hired through the Georgia Tech Research Institute (see separate listing.).
            Thus, this office hires mostly accounting and general management, plus
            positions in public relations, public administration, marketing and fi-
            nance. Experience in higher education desirable. Hires approximately 15
            recent grads and 60 experienced exempt annually. Expects an increase in
            total employment to facilitate projected increase in enrollment.
Procedure: Do not send open resume, since they do not have a computerized appli-
            cant filing system. Call the Job Information Line, and if you wish to
            apply for one of those positions, either apply in person or call for
            instructions. Personnel department is located at
            955 Fowler St NW, Atlanta, GA 30332.
            (404) 894-3245 for general information; 894-4592 for Job Information
            Line.

GEORGIA MARBLE CO.
Profile: Atlanta-based corporation involved in the mining of marble and granite,
            which is then crushed and sawed into smaller sizes for end-user needs.
            Employs 80 at Atlanta headquarters, 55 exempt. Hires a few recent grads
            each year in production management and engineering (IE and ME). Hires
            experienced personnel in accounting/finance, sales, production manage-
            ment, engineering and MIS (IBM 38). Also seeks occasional geologist,
            either trainee or experienced.
Procedure: Send resume to Human Resources Manager,
            1201 Roberts Blvd, Bldg 100, Kennesaw, GA 30144-3619.
            (404) 421-6500

GEORGIA-PACIFIC CORPORATION

Profile: Atlanta-based Fortune 50 forest products company, and Atlanta's second largest Fortune 500 corporation. Headquarters employs 2000, with 1100 exempt. Entry-level accountants and sales reps are hired mostly through campus recruiting, and experienced personnel in accounting/finance, sales, engineering, MIS and other corporate staff types are hired throughout the year. Up to 200 exempt employees are hired annually, and they expect in increase in total employment.

Procedure: Send resume to Headquarters Employment Manager,
133 Peachtree St NE, Atlanta, GA 30303.
(404) 521-4008

GEORGIA POWER COMPANY

Profile: Largest electric utility in Georgia and a subsidiary of Atlanta-based Southern Company. Employs 5000+ in Atlanta, with 2000 exempt. Will hire 100+ recent grads, mostly engineers and other technical degrees; most non-technical positions (accounting, marketing and management) require business major. Also will hire 50+ experienced exempt, mostly with technical backgrounds.

Procedure: Send resume to Professional Employment,
P O Box 4545, Atlanta, GA 30302.
(404) 526-7665

GEORGIA STATE UNIVERSITY

Profile: Georgia's second largest and Atlanta's largest university, with more than 20,000 students, graduate and undergraduates. Employs 1600 non-faculty personnel, approximately 500 exempt. Hires 12 recent grads, some in accounting, but mostly in student services (counseling, financial aid, etc.). Will hire many experienced personnel, especially in accounting/finance, general management, MIS (Amdahl or Unisys) and a few engineers. Also seeks many "Advisors" (academic aid, counselors, etc.) and trainers. Experience in an academic setting is a definite plus.

Procedure: Best method is to call their Job Information Line and apply for a specific opening, since they receive many resumes and an open resume may not receive much attention; they do not maintain a resume file. If you are in Atlanta, you can apply in person; otherwise, mail your resume with a cover letter indicating for which opening you are applying. The address is Employment Office, University Plaza, Atlanta, GA 30303.
(404) 651-3330 for general information; 651-4270 for Job Information Line.

GEORGIA TECH RESEARCH INSTITUTE

Profile: Operates seven research laboratories: five conduct defense electronics-oriented, one does energy-related (ceramics and super-conductors) and one acts as consultant to Georgia industries. Employs 1300, including 650+ engineers and scientists. Hires 30 recent grads and 70 experienced person-

159

nel, mostly with technical backgrounds, especially EE, but also in ME, physics, chemistry, metallurgy, IE and environmental. Economics lab hires mostly MBA's with industrial experience. Hires no office staff types, such as accountants, which are hired through the University (see listing for Georgia Institute of Technology.).

Procedure: Send resume to Technical Recruiter,
GTRI, Human Resources Department, Atlanta, GA 30332.
(404) 894-3411

GLASROCK HOME HEALTH CARE

Profile: With Division headquarters in Atlanta, Glasrock supplies home health care equipment for rent, sale or lease. Headquarters staff numbers 130, and there are support personnel in other locations. Seldom hires recent grads, but will seek 30 experienced personnel in accounting/finance, management and MIS (DEC), and especially individuals with medical backgrounds (physical therapists, respiratory therapists, etc.).

Procedure: Send resume to Human Resources Department,
2840 Mt. Wilkinson Pkwy, Atlanta, GA 30339.
(404) 433-1800

GRADY HOSPITAL   (Fulton-DeKalb Hospital Authority)

Profile: Atlanta's largest hospital, employing 6,000 total, including part-time. Hires 200+ exempt annually, recent grads and experienced, in accounting/finance, department management and MIS (IBM). Also seeks many health care specialists and food service backgrounds. Seldom needs engineers.

Procedure: Send resume to Manager, Personnel Staffing. If there is a current need for your background, they will send you an application form.
80 Butler St SE, Atlanta, GA 30333
(404) 589-4161

H B O & CO.

Profile: Atlanta-based supplier of hospital information systems, employing 700 at their headquarters location. Hires only a few recent grads, mostly accountants and MIS majors, and will hire 75+ experienced exempt in accounting/finance, sales and MIS; healthcare background is helpful. No engineering function here.

Procedure: Send resume to Human Resources,
301 Perimeter Center North, Atlanta, GA 30346.
(404) 393-6000

HARLAND, JOHN H. CO.

Profile: Corporate Headquarters for the second largest bank stationery (mostly checks) company in the US. Employs 300 in headquarters, plus 650 in manufacturing locally. Will hire 30 recent marketing grads as sales trainees and 10 recent grads into production management; relocation out of Atlanta may be required after training. Experienced personnel are hired in accounting/finance, sales, production and MIS. Good source for Junior Military Officers.

Procedure: Send resume to Senior Recruiter,
P O Box 105250, Atlanta, GA 30348.
(404) 981-9460

HAVERTY FURNITURE CO.

Profile: Corporate headquarters for retail furniture chain, operating 12 stores in Atlanta and 80+ in the SE and SW. Employs 350 in Atlanta, with 100 exempt. Prefers to hire recent BBA's in management and marketing for management and administrative positions, including store management trainees, and then promote from within. Also seeks recent MIS grads and promotes up, but will need a few experienced MIS personnel (IBM 38). Hires only experienced accounting/finance, no entry-level.

Procedure: Send resume to Personnel Director,
866 West Peachtree St NW, Atlanta, GA 30308.
(404) 881-1911

HAYES MICROCOMPUTER PRODUCTS, INC.

Profile: Atlanta-based, privately owned computer periferals company that supplies and supports information management and communications products for personal computers, and controls the majority of the modem market. Although the company declined to reveal any employment statistics or information, published sources indicate their employment is around 625, and I have received resumes of current and former employees who had computer experience prior to employment with Hayes.

Procedure: Send resume to Human Resources--Staffing,
P O Box 105203, Atlanta, GA 30348.
(404) 440-8791

HEWLETT-PACKARD COMPANY

Profile: Southern Region Sales Office, covering 12 states and Puerto Rico, for the fourth largest computer manufacturer. Employs 850 in Atlanta, with 600+ exempt, and nearly all are in sales or sales support. Hires a few recent grads, mostly engineers (EE) and computer science, for sales training. Will hire up to 100 experienced technical salespersons for the region. No accounting/finance here.

Procedure: Send resume to Personnel Department,
2015 South Park Place, Atlanta, GA 30339.
(404) 955-1500

HILTON HOTELS (Atlanta Hilton and Towers)

Profile: With 1250 rooms and 1000 employees, this downtown hotel is Atlanta's third largest. Most hiring is for operations management and food/beverage, and some experience is generally required. Will hire a few accountants annually, recent grads and experienced.

Procedure: If in Atlanta, the Hilton prefers that you apply in person, Monday afternoons or Tuesday/Wednesday mornings. Otherwise, send resume to Employment Manager,
255 Courtland St, Atlanta, GA 30303.
(404) 659-2000

HOME DEPOT, INC.

Profile: Atlanta-based retailer of home improvement and building materials supplies. Currently operates 110 stores in 11 states, and is expanding rapidly. Corporate headquarters employs 750, and expects an increase. Recent grads are hired in accounting/finance and MIS (IBM 3090, Wang and DG systems), although not always in an exempt category. College grads are also hired into the management training program, along with non-degreed personnel. Experienced personnel are sought for accounting/finance and MIS, plus buyers, merchandisers and other personnel with home building products industry experience.

Procedure: For corporate staff positions, send resume to Director of Human Resources,
2727 Paces Ferry Rd NW, Atlanta, GA 30339.
(404) 433-8211
Non-exempt, in-store positions are hired at the individual stores.

IBM CORP.

Profile: World leader in information technology, employing 6200 in Atlanta. Most of IBM's hiring is for recent grads in technical sales and MIS-related positions, although there are a few needs for administrative and sales support personnel. Accounting/finance is handled in NYC, and although there are special programs for MBA's, they too, are not in Atlanta. Engineering grads are hired to go into MIS, not engineering. Although IBM prefers to promote from within, and thus hires relatively few experienced exempt, there are special needs in MIS and for sales backgrounds from competitors or other IBM system experience. All hiring for Atlanta goes through this central office.

Procedure: Send resume to Central Employment,
1 Atlantic Center, 1201 West Peachtree St NE, Suite 500, Atlanta, GA 30367-1200
(404) 877-5200

INSTITUTE OF NUCLEAR POWER

Profile: Atlanta-based trade association, whose members are electric utilities with nuclear interests. INPO's purpose is to strengthen the operational safety of nuclear plants. Most exempt needs are for nuclear experience, especially engineers, but they also have occasional needs for accountants and MIS. Seldom hires recent grads.

Procedure: Send resume to Personnel Supervisor,
11 Circle 75 Pkwy, Suite 1500, Atlanta, GA 30339.
(404) 953-3600

K MART

Profile: Southern region office for US's second largest department store chain, operating 38 stores in metro-Atlanta. Hires almost entirely for entry-level "Assistant Manager Trainee" positions, probably 170 each year, at least 15 of whom will stay in Atlanta--in fact, K Mart tries to keep Atlanta hires in Atlanta permanently! Seldom hires experienced exempt, and all accounting and MIS is at corporate headquarters in Michigan.

Procedure: Send resume to Personnel,
2901 Clifton Rd NE. Atlanta. GA 30029.
(404) 320-2500

KENNESTONE REGIONAL HEALTH CARE SYSTEM

Profile: Two-hospital health care system employing 2750, one-half exempt. Hires recent grads into accounting, administration and MIS (IBM 4381), plus nurses and medical therapists. Seeks experienced personnel for the same areas, plus health care engineers and other specialties.

Procedure: Send resume to Central Personnel,
677 Church St, Marietta, GA 30060.
(404) 426-3161

KENTUCKY FRIED CHICKEN

Profile: World's second largest fast-food chain, subsidiary of PepsiCo, Inc. Operates 85+ units in Atlanta, employing 350 exempt-level, plus support staff at Division Headquarters. Will hire 30 recent grads annually, mostly into operations management; food and beverage majors especially appealing. Anticipates hiring 100 experienced exempt, again mostly operations, but also real estate, marketing and human resources. Most accounting and MIS is handled at corporate headquarters in Louisville, KY.

Procedure: Send resume to Human Resources,
Northpark Town Ctr, Bldg 400, 100 Abernathy Rd, Suite 200, Atlanta, GA 30328.
(404) 668-2440

KIMBERLY-CLARK CORP.

Profile: Headquarters operations for Fortune 500 diversified manufacturer, supplying administrative support to several businesses. Employment is 1300, with 900 exempt. Hires mostly recent grads, mainly into research and engineering (ChE, ME, and EE). Experienced needs are usually filled with transfers from other locations, but will have some openings for biology, chemical and polymer backgrounds, including PhD's.

Procedure: Send resume to Human Resource Services,
1400 Holcombe Bridge Rd, Roswell, GA 30076.
(404) 587-8000

KROGER COMPANY

Profile: Largest supermarket chain in Atlanta, with 60+ stores employing 17,000 total. Most hires are for store management and will hire 60, both trainee and experienced. Occasional need for engineers, mostly EE. No accounting.

Procedure: Send resume to Recruiting Manager,
P O Box 105520, Atlanta, GA 30348.
(404) 496-7467

KUPPENHEIMER MEN'S CLOTHIERS

Profile: Corporate headquarters for subsidiary of Chicago-based Hartmarx, and that manufactures, distributes and retails men's clothing. Headquarters staff numbers 150 with 70 exempt, and growing rapidly. Hiring here is for corporate support-types, including accounting/finance, human resources, MIS (AS/400), advertising/media and merchandising/buying, plus manufacturing management; hires mostly experienced, but some recent grads. All store management hiring is conducted at the stores.

Procedure: Send resume to Human Resources Department,
5720 Peachtree Pkwy, Suite 100, Norcross, GA 30092.
(404) 449-5877

KURT SALMON ASSOCIATES

Profile: Management and engineering consulting firm, mainly in textiles and health care. Hires mostly recent grads and will need 30 new grads each year, mostly IE's, computer science majors and MBA's for their strategy group. A few experienced personnel will be hired for the same areas.

Procedure: Send resume to Recruiting Assistant,
400 Colony Square, Suite 900, Atlanta, GA 30361.
(404) 892-0321

LANIER WORLDWIDE

Profile: Corporate headquarters for subsidiary of Melbourne, FL-based Harris Corp., and formed in 1989 with the merger of Harris's copier sales operations and its Lanier voice (phone systems) and business systems (fax machines) divisions. Employs 1375 in Atlanta, one-half exempt. Most needs are for accounting/finance, recent grad and experienced. Recent grads should have some experience, e.g., co-op or summer jobs. Also hires R&D engineers (EE or CS) and MIS. No manufacturing here. Sales personnel are hired at the field offices.

164

Procedure: Send resume to Corporate Recruiter,
2300 Parklake Dr NE, Atlanta, GA 30345.
(404) 496-9500

LAW ENGINEERING/LAW & COMPANY
Profile: Atlanta-based engineering consulting firm, primarily for the construction industry. Employs 400 at corporate headquarters, including 200 exempt. Definitely expects increase in employment. Hires mostly recent grads and promotes from within. Will hire 50 engineers, mostly civil and construction-related, and a few in accounting. Will hire only a few experienced exempt, mostly in accounting, engineering and technical or industrial sales.
Procedure: Send resume to Corporate Personnel Manager,
P O Box 888013, Atlanta, GA 30359.
(404) 396-8000

LAW ENVIRONMENTAL
Profile: Atlanta-based environmental consulting firm, subsidiary of Law & Co. Employs 400 in Atlanta, with 125+ exempt, and expects an increase. Will hire 80 exempt personnel, recent grads and experienced, in all areas (accounting/finance, sales, administration, engineering and MIS), especially environment-related technical backgrounds.
Procedure: Send resume to Corporate Recruiter,
112 Town Park Dr, Kennesaw, GA 30144.
(404) 421-3400

LIFE OF GEORGIA
Profile: Largest Atlanta-based life and health insurance company, rated A+ by Best Reports. Will undergo rapid increase in employment in 1990, from 850 now to 1100+ by mid-year. Will hire 75 recent grads and 80 experienced exempt in underwriting, management, claims, accounting/finance, and MIS (IBM 3090).
Procedure: Send resume to Personnel Department,
5780 Powers Ferry Rd NW, Atlanta, GA 30327-4390.
(404) 980-5710

LITHONIA LIGHTING
Profile: Corporate headquarters for national manufacturer of all types of lighting fixtures for residential, commercial and industrial uses. Largest subsidiary of National Service Industries, Atlanta-based Fortune 500 corporation. Employs 2200 in Atlanta, with 250 exempt. Hires recent grads as marketing and manufacturing trainees, plus 20+ experienced personnel in all corporate and manufacturing functions.
Procedure: Send resume to Corporate Manager,
1135 Industrial Blvd, Conyers, GA 30207.

(404) 922-9000

LOCKHEED GEORGIA CO.
Profile: For many years Atlanta's largest employer, Lockheed has been down-siz-
ing, and anticipates no needs for additional personnel.

LOCKWOOD GREENE
Profile: Headquartered in Spartanburg, SC, this consulting firm is involved primarily in the design of large industrial projects. Also acts as designers,
architects, managers and planners of major commercial, institutional and
industrial facilities. Employs 600 in Atlanta, a 64% growth over 1988,
and anticipates a further increase during 1990! Will hire 10+ recent grads,
mostly engineers (ME, EE, CE and ChE--no IE), and 120 experienced
engineers and designers with experience in the design of large industrial
projects. Hires six co-op engineers each year.
Procedure: Send resume to Manager, Personnel and Administration,
1330 West Peachtree St NW, Atlanta, GA 30367.
(404) 873-3261

LORAL INFORMATION DISPLAY SYSTEMS
Profile: Corporate headquarters for company that designs, develops and manufactures information display systems for military applications. Employs
200+ and expects sharp increase in employment. Hires no recent grads,
but will hire experienced personnel in accounting/finance, engineering
(mostly EE), MIS (uses PC's) and manufacturing management.
Procedure: Send resume to Director of Personnel,
6765 Peachtree Industrial Blvd, Atlanta, GA 30360.
(404) 448-1604

M & M PRODUCTS CO.
Profile: Corporate headquarters for the tenth largest black-owned US company and
third largest manufacturer of ethnic hair care products. Rarely hires recent
grads, but seeks experienced personnel in manufacturing management,
MIS (IBM 38), research and marketing. No sales force and seldom needs
engineers.
Procedure: Send resume to Director of Personnel,
P O Box 16549, Atlanta, GA 30321.
(404) 366-1717

MARTA (Metropolitan Atlanta Rapid Transit Authority)
Profile: Employs 3700 with one-third exempt, mostly at headquarters. Will begin
hiring recent grads in 1990, mostly in accounting, engineering and MIS
(IBM 380). Most hiring will be for experienced exempt in account-
ing/finance, administration and staff support management, engineering

166

(construction, CE, structural, ME, EE and specialized), MIS and human resources specialties.

Procedure: Send resume to Director of Personnel,
2424 Piedmont Rd NE, Atlanta, GA 30324-3324.
(404) 848-5544 for information; 848-5231 for recording on hiring procedure and current vacancies.

MCI TELECOMMUNICATIONS CORP

Profile: Second largest telephone long distance service provider, employing 1600 in Atlanta with 800+ exempt. Hires only a few recent grads, but will hire 80+ experienced exempt, mostly in accounting/finance, sales, telecommunication and MBA's.

Procedure: Send resume to Employment,
400 Perimeter Center Terrace, Suite 400, Atlanta, GA 30346.
(404) 668-6535

MACY'S SOUTH/BULLOCK'S

Profile: Parent company of Macy's, one of Atlanta's two largest department store chains, this office handles hiring for a 45-store chain of department stores stretching from South Carolina to California. Has personnel needs in all areas, for both recent grads and experienced exempt, plus retail specialties.

Procedure: Employs numerous recruiters handling specific areas, but a resume simply sent to "Human Resources" will be directed to the appropriate recruiter.
180 Peachtree St NW, Atlanta, GA 30303
(404) 221-7641

MANAGEMENT SCIENCE AMERICA, INC. (MSA)

Profile: Atlanta-based corporation that designs and manufactures business software systems in finance, human resources, manufacturing and higher education. Employs 1000 in Atlanta with 750 exempt. Will hire 300 exempt (not all for Atlanta) in accounting/finance, MIS (IBM) and sales (no trainees).

Procedure: Send resume to Director of Recruiting,
3445 Peachtree Rd NE, Atlanta, GA 30326.
(404) 239-2000

MICROBILT

Profile: Atlanta-based, high-tech company, recently acquired by First Financial Management Company (see separate listing). Provides data communications network (e.g., electronic mail, credit card terminals, electronic forms, electronic interfacing, etc.). Will hire 25± personnel, both recent grads and experienced, in all areas.

Procedure: Send resume to Personnel Department,
P O Box 723368, Atlanta, GA 30339.
(404) 955-0313

MOBIL CHEMICAL COMPANY
Profile: Manufactures and sells polyethylene (plastic films) and polystyrene (plastic foam) disposable products for consumer, industrial and institutional use. Consumer brand names include Baggies and Hefty. This manufacturing and distribution facility employs 800 total, with 85 exempt. Hires few recent grads, but will hire 15-20 experienced exempt in accounting/finance, sales, manufacturing and distribution management, and engineering. Also has occasional need for MBA's and human resources.

Procedure: Send resume to Employee Relations,
P O Box 71, Covington, GA 30209.
(404) 786-5372

NCR--Engineering and Manufacturing/Atlanta
Profile: Designs, develops and manufactures integrated software and hardware computer systems for retailers. New center, with employment projections of 400 (325 exempt) by the end of 1990. NCR's corporate policy is to hire 95% recent grads and promote from within. Most of their needs will be for engineers (computer and EE) and computer science majors, plus a few general business grads. Offers 30 summer internships.

Procedure: Send resume to Personnel Resources,
2651 Satellite Blvd., Duluth, GA 30136.
(404) 441-8100 (may change)

NCR CORP.--U S Data Processing Group
Profile: Largest NCR division and marketing group, employing 16,000+ in US and 1300 in Atlanta, 500+ exempt. Provides marketing and staff support for their sales organization. Hires many recent grads annually in accounting/finance, sales, management and MIS. No needs for engineers.

Procedure: Send resume to Region Personnel Manager,
P O Box 4704, Norcross, GA 30091.
(404) 441-8370, but do not call; they always respond to resumes, usually within two weeks.

NCR-- Worldwide Service Parts Center
Profile: Facility that handles national and international distribution of NCR parts. Employs 640 total, 150+ exempt. Hires mostly recent grads in engineering (EE), programming (NCR hardware) and purchasing agents (BBA best). Will also need a few experienced personnel, especially purchasing.

Procedure: Send resume to Personnel Administrator,
259 Highway 74 South, Peachtree City, GA 30269.
(404) 487-7000

NEC HOME ELECTRONICS USA, INC.

Profile: Manufacturer of color TV's, projection TV's, portable computers and computer monitors. Employs 650 with 100 exempt, and expecting an increase. Hires no recent grads, but will seek 25 experienced exempt in accounting, MIS (NEC system), manufacturing management and engineering (mostly ME and design).

Procedure: Send resume to Manager of Human Resources, 1 NEC Drive, McDonough, GA 30253. (404) 957-6600

NATIONAL DATA CORP.

Profile: Atlanta-based data processing company within the computer services industry, providing data exchange, processing and telecommunications services to a variety of financial and corporate clients. Employs 2000, 1000 exempt and anticipates hiring 200 exempt in 1990. Recent grads are hired mostly as programmers and customer service representatives (BBA or liberal arts). Experienced exempt are hired in a variety of areas: customer service; programming and all types of MIS professionals; engineers (EE, EET and MET); accountants and financial analysts; sales representatives with experience in banking (cash management or credit cards especially), health care software systems and telecommunications.

Procedure: Send resume to Director of Employment, NDC Plaza, Atlanta, GA 30329. (404) 728-2000

NATIONAL LINEN SERVICE

Profile: Atlanta-based division of Fortune 500 National Service Industries, also headquartered in Atlanta (see next listing). This is the textile rental division, mostly apparel, and is NSI's second largest division, employing 9000 nationwide. However, most of these employees are not in Atlanta, and thus they have limited opportunities here. Will need recent grads in accounting/finance and for their Management Development Program (production-oriented). Also will seek a few experienced production processing managers and sales representatives.

Procedure: Send resume to Personnel Specialist, 1420 Peachtree St, Atlanta, GA 30309. (404) 853-1000

NATIONAL SERVICE INDUSTRIES

Profile: Corporate headquarters for this Fortune 500 corporation, divided into seven divisions, which operate autonomously and handle their own hiring. Thus, NSI headquarters employs very few, and their personnel needs are handled by National Linen Service's personnel department. (See National Linen Service, Lithonia Lighting and Zep Manufacturing Co.)

Procedure: Same as above.

NORDSON CORPORATION
Profile: North American Division Headquarters of Ohio-based Nordson Corp, a major manufacturer of finishing and adhesive application equipment. This office provides marketing and technical support for several Nordson groups. Employs 200+ total, with one-half exempt, and expects an increase. Seldom hires recent grads, but seeks experienced exempt in sales, engineering (ME, EE), marketing specialties (analysts, product development, etc.) and technical training.
Procedure: Send resume to Manager, Human Resources,
               350 Research Court, Norcross, GA 30092.
               (404) 449-7570

NORRELL CORP.
Profile: Corporate headquarters for the fifth largest temporary help company in the US. Operates 20 branches in Atlanta, 300+ nationally. Corporate headquarters employs 300, with 30% exempt. Will hire a few recent grads and 30+ experienced exempt in accounting/finance, sales and sales management, MIS and marketing.
Procedure: Send resume to Corporate Recruiter,
               3535 Piedmont Rd NE, Atlanta, GA 30305.
               (404) 262-2100

NORTHERN TELECOM
Profile: Canadian-based manufacturer of telecommunications transmissions equipment. Employs 1100 in Atlanta with one-third exempt. Hires mostly EE's, plus a few accountants and other disciplines, both recent grads and experienced. Expanding marketing department, and will seek experienced specialists there.
Procedure: Send resume to Staffing Manager,
               1555 Roadhaven Dr, Stone Mountain, GA 30083.
               (404) 491-7717

OGILVY & MATHER
Profile: One of Atlanta's largest ad agencies, headquartered in NYC. Employs 85 in Atlanta with 70 exempt. Hires a limited number of recent grads with experience or internship with an ad agency. Also hires experienced advertising professionals, and prefers ad experience for accountants. Offers several internships year-round for college advertising majors.
Procedure: Send resume to Personnel Manager,
               1360 Peachtree St NE, Atlanta, GA 30309.
               (404) 888-5100

OKI TELECOM
Profile: Manufactures and sells switchgear and switchboard apparatus for telecommunications industry. Employs 500 with 60 exempt. Most needs (recent grads and experienced) are for engineers (EE, IE, ME and software), plus occasional accountant.

Procedure: Send resume to Human Resources Department,
            437 Old Peachtree Rd, Suwanee, GA 30174.
            (404) 995-9800

OXFORD INDUSTRIES
Profile: Atlanta-based, Fortune 500 apparel manufacturing and marketing company, mostly for private and contract labels. Has manufacturing facilities throughout the Southeast, including several close to Atlanta. Corporate staff numbers 250, 60% exempt. Hires mostly recent grads in accounting, manufacturing management, MIS and sales (may be transferred to NYC later). Also seeks experienced MIS.

Procedure: Send resume to Director of Employment and Training,
            222 Piedmont Ave NE, Atlanta, GA 30308.
            (404) 659-2424

PANASONIC   (Matsushita Communication Corp of America)
Profile: Facility that manufactures cash registers and order-taking equipment, plus cellular phones, pagers and car stereos. Employs 530 (100+ exempt) and expecting an increase. Will hire 10 recent grads in design engineering, plus experienced exempt in accounting, production management and design engineering.

Procedure: Send resume to Personnel,
            776 Hwy 74 South, Peachtree City, GA 30269.
            (404) 487-3356

PANASONIC   (Matsushita Electric Corp of America)
Profile: Southeast region sales and service office, employing 300+. Will hire an occasional recent accounting grad, and will need experienced consumer and industrial sales reps.

Procedure: Send resume to Recruiter,
            1854 Shackleford Ct, Norcross, GA 30093.
            (404) 925-6700

PEAT MARWICK MAIN & CO.
Profile: Fourth largest CPA firm in Atlanta, one of the "Big 6" international CPA firms. Audit and tax are the largest divisions; consulting is relatively small. Employs 420 total with 360 exempt, and expects an increase. 85% of new hires (total 45/yr) will be recent accounting/finance grads and MBA's (no recent MIS grads). Likes tax MAcc grads.

Procedure: Send resume to Director of Personnel,

235 Peachtree Center Ave, Suite 1900, Atlanta, GA 30343.
(404) 577-3240

PENNEY, J. C. & COMPANY

Profile: Region headquarters for nation's fourth largest retail chain, specializing in soft lines. Only recruiting is for store management, especially recent grads to enter training program. All accounting and MIS is at corporate headquarters in Dallas, TX.

Procedure: Much entry-level hiring is done through campus recruiting, but resumes are accepted also. Send resume to Personnel,
715 Peachtree St NE, Atlanta, GA 30302.
(404) 897-5500

PENNEY'S CATALOGUE DISTRIBUTION CENTER

Profile: One of six national distribution centers, employing 2400, with 150 exempt. Almost all hiring is for Management Trainees in operations and distribution, and then promoted up.

Procedure: Send resume to Employment and Personnel Relations Manager,
90 Annex, Atlanta, GA 30390.
(404) 361-7700

PEPSICO EMPLOYMENT PLUS

Profile: New venture by PepsiCo to consolidate the recruiting functions of their three fast food subsidiaries--Pizza Hut, Kentucky Fried Chicken and Taco Bell. This office recruits primarily for the Atlanta needs of those three, mostly restaurant managers (recent grads and experienced), but also for finance MBA's (recent grads should be from top school) and experienced real estate site selectors and human resources specialists.

Procedure: Send resume to Personnel,
1395 Marietta Pkwy, Bldg 300, Suite 210, Marietta, GA 30067.
(404) 429-7770

PIZZA HUT

Profile: Third largest fast food chain in the world, subsidiary of Pepsico, Inc. Operates 125 stores in the Atlanta area. Most hiring here is for store operations and management, probably 30 recent grads and 125 experienced.

Procedure: Send resume to Human Resources,
400 Northridge Road, Suite 600, Atlanta, GA 30350.
(404) 998-7272

PORTMAN COMPANIES

Profile: Atlanta-based parent company of internationally renown architect John Portman. This office employs 800 and handles commercial real estate design, development, management and finance. No recruiting function as part of the Human Resources Department; rather, HR acts as a clearing house or liaison with various departments, and refers resumes to the appropriate hiring source. Most experienced exempt positions are very specialized, and they rely heavily on in-house job postings, referrals and personnel agency contacts. Recent grads are hired in accounting, plus there are numerous needs in their marketing department for journalists and communications majors.

Procedure: Send resume to Human Resources,
225 Peachtree St NE, Suite 201, Atlanta, GA 30303.
(404) 420-5252

RACETRAC PETROLEUM, INC.

Profile: Corporate headquarters for retail gas and convenience store chain. Headquarters staff numbers 230, with 70 exempt. Hires a few recent accounting grads, but most needs are for exempt personnel in accounting/finance, marketing, construction, legal and MIS (IBM 38 and AS 400).

Procedure: Send resume to Personnel Manager,
300 Technology Court, Smyrna, GA 30082.
(404) 431-7600

RICH'S DEPARTMENT STORES

Profile: Corporate headquarters for one of the two largest department store chains in Atlanta, and division of Federated Department Stores. Employs 10,000 in Atlanta. Most recent grads are needed for their "Executive Training Program," which encompasses all facets of the corporation. Experienced exempt hired are mostly accounting/finance, retail professionals and MBA's for sales support group. Most MIS functions are handled by SABRE Group (see listing).

Procedure: Send resume to Executive Recruitment Staff,
45 Broad St, Atlanta, GA 30302.
(404) 586-2230

ROBINSON-HUMPHREY COMPANY, INC.

Profile: Full-service financial services firm, specializing in the southeast region, selling institutional and individual investment opportunities. Corporate headquartered in Atlanta and subsidiary of Shearson Lehman Hutton. Employs 600 in Atlanta. Recent grads are not hired as brokers, unless they have three years prior sales experience. Hires 10 recent grads each year, mostly MBA's, finance or economics majors, to be "Corporate Financial Analysts" or other analytical position. Some recent grads start in the Mail Room (!!!) or other similar position, to learn business basics. Will hire 25 experienced exempt in the same areas, plus brokers (three years of any sales experience required). No formal training program.

Procedure: Send resume to Director of Human Resources,
3333 Peachtree Rd NE, 7th Floor, Atlanta, GA 30326.
(404) 266-6000

ROCKWELL INTERNATIONAL--Missile Systems Division
Profile: Major defense contractor, manufacturing high-tech components. Employs 1600 with 700 exempt. Hires 100+ each year, both recent grads and experienced exempt, primarily for engineering (EE mostly). There are also needs for experienced accounting/finance and others with DOD experience.
Procedure: Send resume with cover letter indicating job objective and areas of expertise to Human Resources--Employment,
             1800 Satellite Blvd, Duluth, GA 30136.
             (404) 476-6460

ROLLINS, INC.
Profile: Corporate headquarters for diversified service corporation, including Orkin Exterminating Company and Rollins Protective Services. Employs 500 with 200 exempt. Hires 80 exempt annually. Recent grads hired are usually entry accountants. Seeks experienced personnel for typical corporate headquarters types: sales, accounting/finance, insurance administration, distribution, etc.
Procedure: Send resume to Employment Director,
             2170 Piedmont Rd NE, Atlanta, GA 30324.
             (404) 888-2000

RUSSELL, H. J. & CO.
Profile: Fourth largest black-owned business in the US, headquartered in Atlanta. Has eight subsidiaries, primarily in real estate, construction and communications. Employs 450 in Atlanta office, with 40% exempt. Hires few recent grads, except for their interns. Experienced personnel hired include accounting/finance, property management, construction engineers, management services (*i.e.*, personnel, PR, administration, etc.) and MIS (IBM 34).
Procedure: Send resume to Human Resources Director,
             504 Fair St SW, Atlanta, GA 30313.
             (404) 330-1000

SABRE GROUP, THE
Profile: Atlanta-based information processing division of Allied/Federated department stores, parent of Atlanta-based Rich's department stores and others. Employs 600, and nearly all recruitment is for MIS, recent grads and experienced. They operate three IBM 3090's.
Procedure: Send resume to Personnel,
             6620 Bay Circle, Norcross, GA 30071.
             (404) 448-8900

SALES TECHNOLOGIES

Profile: Corporate headquarters in Atlanta and subsidiary of D&B, Sales Tech-
            nologies was Atlanta's fastest growing high-tech company in 1988. De-
            signs, develops, installs, markets and supports software to improve pro-
            ductivity of large sales forces. Employs 220 here, and anticipates an in-
            crease. Nearly all exempt needs are in MIS, some recent Computer Sci-
            ence grads, but mostly for experienced DEC VAX professionals and
            experienced "C" programmers.
Procedure: Send resume to Supervisor, Employment,
            3399 Peachtree Rd NE, Suite 700, Atlanta, GA 30326.
            (404) 841-4000

SCHLUMBERGER INDUSTRIES--Sangamo Electricity Division

Profile: Division headquarters, manufactures electrical measurement and control
            products for use by the public utility industry. Will hire 15+ recent grads
            annually, mostly engineers (EE, MIS-related) and computer science back-
            grounds for applications, software and hardware design. Also seeks up to
            15 experienced personnel in the same areas, plus sales engineers.
Procedure: Send resume to Personnel Department,
            180 Technology Pkwy, Norcross, GA 30092.
            (404) 447-7300

SCIENTIFIC ATLANTA

Profile: Fortune 500 corporation and largest high-tech company headquartered in
            Atlanta. Manufactures and distributes communications products, defense
            systems and test instruments. Employs 2000+ in Atlanta, one-half ex-
            empt level. Will hire 200+ new employees (recent grads and experienced)
            annually, and in all corporate areas, including accounting/finance,
            engineering, marketing, planning, sales, MBA's and "misc. professional."
Procedure: Send resume to Professional Employment,
            P O Box 105027, Atlanta, GA 30348.
            (404) 441-4000

SIEMENS ENERGY & AUTOMATION

With US Corporate Headquarters in Atlanta, the company is a subsidiary of Munich,
Germany-based Siemens AG, one of the largest international firms. Siemens' various
offices in Atlanta employ 2000+, and offer a wide variety of electrical and electronic
equipment and systems. In addition to the corporate headquarters facility here, there are
several divisions also headquartered in Atlanta, and each handles its own employment.
The most active employment centers are listed below:

Siemens/Atlanta Area Service Center

Profile: Manufactures commercial switchboards and panelboards. Employs 250
            total with 40 exempt. Hires recent engineering grads (EE and ME), and
            has two co-op engineering students. Hires experienced exempt in ac-
            counting, engineering (EE and ME), MIS (Prime) and materials manage-
            ment.

Procedure: Send resume to Manager of Employee Relations,
2140 Flintstone Drive, Tucker, GA 30085.
(404) 491-3940

Siemens/Automation Division
Profile: Manufactures AC and DC variable speed drives, programmable control
products, industrial systems, power systems, and transportation traction
systems. Most hires are for engineers (EE and electrical related), recent
grads and experienced.
Procedure: Send resume to Human Resources,
150 Hembree Park Dr, Roswell, GA 30077
(404) 442-2500
Note: This division is moving into new headquarters facility on Georgia
Hwy 400 during 1990.

Siemens Energy & Automation--Corporate Headquarters
Profile: Hires recent grads in accounting/finance, engineering (mostly EE, ME and
IE), MIS (need CS degree), and management. Has two-year Management
Training program in accounting/finance or engineering: employee is
given four six-month assignments and then permanent assignment, based
on results of temporary assignments. Will also seek experienced exempt
in same areas, although most engineers are hired at division level (see
listings below). Has need for German bilingual applicants, and offers exchange program to send middle-management personnel for assignments in
Munich headquarters.
Procedure: Send resume to Corporate Personnel Manager,
P O Box 89000, Atlanta, GA 30356.
(404) 751-2000

Siemens/Circuit Protection Division
Profile: Manufactures and sells low voltage electrical distribution equipment for
commercial, industrial and residential uses. Hires a few recent grads, plus
25± experienced personnel in accounting/finance, engineering (all types)
and marketing analysis.
Procedure: Send resume to Employee Relations,
3333 State Bridge Rd, Alpharetta, GA 30201.
(404) 751-2000

SIMONS-EASTERN CONSULTANTS
Profile: Atlanta-based, multi-discipline design and consulting firm, specializing in
the design of paper mills. Employs 1000 total, 850 exempt, and expects
an increase. Most personnel needs are for engineers and designers (CE,
ChE, ME, EE and pulp and paper), some recent grads but mostly experienced. Also hires some experienced exempt in accounting/finance, MIS
and personnel. Has co-op programs for engineering students.
Procedure: Send resume to Personnel,
P O Box 1286, Atlanta, GA 30301.
(404) 370-3200

SMITH, W. H. USA
Profile: US Corporate Headquarters of British conglomerate. Owns and operates 300+ retail gift shops located in airports, hotels and office buildings nationwide. Employs 250 in Atlanta, with 100 exempt. Hires recent grads for accounting, a few MIS (DG system) and Manager Trainees. Hires experienced accounting/finance, distribution managers, marketing/advertising, buyers, merchandisers and MIS.
Procedure: For Manager Trainee, send resume to Regional Manager; for other positions, send resume to Personnel Coordinator,
2141 Powers Ferry Rd, Suite 300, Marietta, GA 30067.
(404) 952-0705

SNAPPER POWER EQUIPMENT
Profile: Atlanta-based manufacturer of outdoor power equipment (mostly for lawn and garden), and subsidiary of Atlanta-based Fuqua Industries. Employs 650, with 225 exempt. Hires numerous recent grads in all areas; also likes to hire recent grads into non-exempt positions to learn business "from ground up," and then promote to exempt positions. Hires experienced personnel in all areas, especially manufacturing backgrounds.
Procedure: Send resume to Personnel Department,
P O Box 777, McDonough, GA 30253.
(404) 957-9141

SOUTHERN BELL
(see BellSouth)

SOUTHERN COMPANY SERVICES
Profile: Provides accounting/finance and MIS assistance to subsidiary power companies throughout the Southeast, including Georgia Power. Employs 1200 (700 in MIS-related), with 800 exempt. Hires 50± recent grads annually (3.0 GPA preferred), and a few experienced exempt, almost entirely in MIS (IBM backgrounds best), plus some accounting/finance, PR/communications and other headquarters types.
Procedure: Hires heavily through campus recruiting, and prefers you not send unsolicited resume. Check first with their Job Hot Line, then respond to a specific opening. Send resume to Personnel Department,
64 Perimeter Center East, Atlanta, GA 30346.
(404) 393-0650; 668-3464 - Job Hot Line

SOUTHWIRE
Profile: Corporate headquarters for the nation's largest manufacturer of rod, wire and cable. Employs 2750 at this location, with 500 exempt. Will hire 20 recent grads and 20 experienced exempt in all areas, including account-

ing/finance, sales, management, MIS and especially engineering. Also hires 10 co-op students each year.

Procedure: Send resume to Professional Employment,
P O Box 1000, Carrollton, GA 30119.
(404) 577-3280

SUNTRUST BANKS, INC.

Profile: Corporate headquartered in Atlanta, SunTrust is the third largest SE-based bank holding company, and controls several SE banks, including Atlanta's Trust Company Banks. All hiring is conducted through the personnel department of Trust Company Bank.

Procedure: See Trust Company Bank.

SUNTRUST SERVICES

Profile: Handles programming operations for Trust Company Bank and SunTrust. Employs 250 and anticipates hiring 15 recent grads (prefers Computer Science major) and 20 experienced MIS professionals annually.

Procedure: Send resume to Employment Manager,
P O Box 4418, Atlanta, GA 30302.
(404) 588-8877

TELECOM*USA

Profile: Corporate headquarters for the nation's fourth largest long-distance communications carrier, employing 400+ in Atlanta. Expanding rapidly, primarily through acquisition. Hires recent grads in accounting and engineering (all types), and experienced exempt in same areas, plus sales and marketing. No MIS here; MIS is hired for their operations center in Greenville, SC.

Procedure: Send resume to Human Resources Manager,
780 Douglas Rd, Suite 800, Atlanta, GA 30342.
(404) 250-5500

THOMPSON, J. WALTER

Profile: Third largest advertising agency in the world, and one of the largest in Atlanta. Employs 125 total, with 80% exempt. Rarely hires recent grads, but will hire experienced accounting/finance and other advertising professionals with 1+ years experience.

Procedure: Send resume to Personnel,
1 Atlanta Plaza, 950 E. Paces Ferry Rd NE, Atlanta, GA 30326.
(404) 365-7300

TRANSUS, INC.

Profile: Southeastern common carrier and transportation service, corporate headquartered in Atlanta. Hires recent grads and experienced personnel for accounting/finance, operations management, sales, MIS (IBM 4381) and technical school grads.

Procedure: Send resume to Employment Office,
2090 Jonesboro Rd, Atlanta, GA 30315.
(404) 627-7331

TRUST COMPANY BANK
Profile: Second largest bank in Georgia in assets and subsidiary of Atlanta-based SunTrust Banks (see separate listing). Employs 4800 in Atlanta. Recent grads are hired primarily from February through April, and those interested in a banking career can enter their "Commercial Banking Training Program." Experienced personnel are hired all year, and there are needs in all areas, especially accounting/finance, MIS, banking professionals, etc.

Procedure: Send resume to Employment Manager,
P O Box 4418, Atlanta, GA 30302.
(404) 588-7199

TUCKER WAYNE/LUCKIE & CO.
Profile: Atlanta-headquartered and largest privately-owned advertising agency in Atlanta. Employs 125 and hires only experienced advertising professionals. Seldom needs accounting or MIS.

Procedure: Has no centralized resume distribution system, and each department head hires for his/her area only. Thus, send resume to a specific functional area (e.g., creative or research), or simply to the company and it will be handed to the appropriate person.

TURNER BROADCASTING SYSTEM, INC.
Corporate headquarters for the broadcasting empire of well-known Ted Turner, TBS is a cable programmer (four channels) and syndicator of programs, including SuperStation 17. TBS employs 2000+ in Atlanta, and strongly prefers to hire entry-level (frequently non-exempt) and then promote from within, although there are some needs for experienced exempt personnel. The three broadcast companies each offer internships for juniors, seniors and recent grads. Their four autonomous hiring offices are listed below. (TBS has a central mail room, and thus you will notice three offices have the same address.)

Cable News Network
Profile: Operates a 24-hour cable news gathering organization, which includes CNN, CNN headlines and CNN radio. Hires 40 recent grads annually, but requires broadcast and/or internship experience. Only experienced personnel hired have 3-7 years live TV experience.

Procedure: Send resume to Personnel,
1 CNN Center, P O Box 105366, Atlanta, GA 30348-5366.
(404) 827-1500

TBS Engineering Department

179

Profile: Provides engineering services for entire company. Hires 12± recent BS and AS grads (EET and MET mostly) to work in quality control engineering and maintenance. Also needs 12± experienced engineers annually, preferably with broadcast experience.

Procedure: Send resume to Engineering Training Director,
1 CNN Center, P O Box 105366, Atlanta, GA 30348-5366.
(404) 827-1700 x1638

Turner Broadcasting System

Profile: Corporate headquarters location, and hires more experienced exempt than other hiring offices, mostly in accounting/finance, sales (TV time sales and cable) and MIS. Hires recent grads in accounting, usually as non-exempt, then promotes through in-house posting system.

Procedure: Send resume with cover letter including areas of interest and expertise to Personnel Department,
1 CNN Center, P O Box 105366, Atlanta, GA 30348-5366.
(404) 827-1700, but do not call. No information is given by phone.

Turner Network Television

Profile: Came on-air in October, 1988, and is the entertainment cable operation. Like CNN, TNT seeks mostly recent grads or other entry-level personnel with TV intern experience, especially in the entertainment sector. Also conducts hiring for SuperStation Channel 17.

Procedure: Send resume to Personnel Administrator,
1050 Techwood Dr NW, Atlanta, GA 30348.
(404) 827-1111

U S SPRINT COMMUNICATIONS CO -- National Accounts Division

Profile: Third largest long distance telephone carrier, and this office provides telecommunications sales and marketing support to large, national corporations. Employs 500 total with 375 exempt, and an increase in employment is projected. Hires no recent grads, but will hire up to 100 exempt personnel with sales, marketing or technical experience in telecommunications or any other large system (e.g., computers).

Procedure: Send resume to Staffing Manager,
3100 Cumberland Circle, Atlanta, GA 30339.
(404) 859-5000

U S SPRINT COMMUNICATIONS CO. -- Southeast Division

Profile: Provides technical support to US Sprint, and services non-national accounts (i.e., residential and small- to medium-sized businesses). Employs 800, with 350 exempt. Expects to hire 50 recent grads and 100 experienced exempt in credit, customer service, telemarketing, network engineering and MIS (IBM). No accounting/finance needs here.

Procedure: Send resume to Human Resources Department,
3065 Hargrove Rd, Atlanta, GA 30339. Or you can go by their office to review their list of current needs, and then apply for a specific opening.

(404) 859-8000

UNITED FAMILY LIFE INSURANCE CO.
Profile: Atlanta-based life insurance company, employs 225 at headquarters, plus 1000+ sales reps. Primary hiring is for experienced insurance specialties (claims, underwriting, etc.) and department managers; seldom hires recent grads. Small, stable accounting and MIS staff.
Procedure: Send resume to Personnel Department,
P O Box 2204, Atlanta, GA 30371.
(404) 659-3300

UPTON'S DEPARTMENT STORES
Profile: Corporate headquarters for this privately-held apparel chain, operating 23 stores in the Southeast and nine in Atlanta. Seeks both recent grads and experienced personnel (probably 75+ per year) in accounting/finance, management, MBA's and MIS (IBM 38). Also seeks experienced buyers, retail managers and personnel managers. Expects increase in employment.
Procedure: Send resume to Manager of Recruitment,
6356 Corley Rd, Norcross, GA 30071.
(404) 662-2500

WANG LABORATORIES
Profile: An international leader in data communications, Wang is currently downsizing its Atlanta staff, and expects to employ 250 at this office by the beginning of 1990, with 125 exempt. Wang will hire a few recent grads into sales training, and will need experienced exempt in accounting/finance, sales, administration, technical support and hardware support, especially from other data processing companies.
Procedure: Send resume to Human Resources,
900 Ashwood Pkwy, 8th Floor, Atlanta, GA 30338.
(404) 392-5700

WANG LABORATORIES -- Regional Support Center
Profile: Supplies MIS support to other Wang Components. Hires mostly MIS personnel, both recent grad and experienced. Employs 215 with 100+ exempt, and expects an increase in employment.
Procedure: Send resume to Human Resources Manager,
2300 Lake Park Dr, Smyrna, GA 30080.
(404) 436-9001

WENDY'S OLD FASHIONED HAMBURGERS
Profile: Fourth largest fast food chain in the world, Wendy's operates 100+ units in Georgia, employing 6000. Plans to hire 25 recent grads and 125

experienced exempt into operations management, plus a few experienced accountants.

Procedure: Send resume to Human Resources Representative,
375 Franklin Rd, Suite 400, Marietta, GA 30067.
(404) 587-5229

WEST BUILDING MATERIALS

Profile: Atlanta-based retailer and supplier of building materials, operating 18 stores in Atlanta and 70+ stores nationally. Employs 1200± in Atlanta, including 300 in headquarters. Corporate needs will be for accounting/finance, sales, administrative and MIS (recent grads and experienced)--probably 25 annually.

Procedure: Send resume to Personnel,
P O Box 7187, Station C, Atlanta, GA 30309.
(404) 894-7800

WILKINSON SWORD

Profile: Atlanta-based manufacturer and distributor of razors, shave cream and cutlery; subsidiary of Swedish STORA company. Employs 200 at headquarters and anticipates an increase. Hires no recent grads, but has summer internships. Most experienced exempt hired are for accounting/finance and MIS (IBM).

Procedure: Send resume to Human Resources Department,
7012 Best Friend Rd, Atlanta, GA 30340.
(404) 441-3030

WILLIAMS, A. L. CORPORATION

Profile: Atlanta-based company selling term life insurance and mutual funds, employing 1900 at headquarters. Seeks recent grads and experienced exempt in all areas (except engineering), especially insurance specialties.

Procedure: Send resume to Corporate Employment Center, attn: Corporate Recruiter,
3120 Breckinridge Blvd, Duluth, GA 30199-0001.
(404) 381-1674

XEROX CORP.

Profile: District office for sales of office equipment and machinery. Hires recent grads and experienced exempt, primarily for sales positions.

Procedure: Send resume to Senior Recruiting Coordinator,
1 Concourse Pkwy, Suite 800, Atlanta, GA 30328.
(404) 395-2000

ZEP MANUFACTURING CO.

Profile: Corporate headquarters in Atlanta, third largest and most profitable sub-
              sidiary of Atlanta-based National Service Industries (see separate listing).
              Manufactures and sells specialty chemicals for the maintenance industry.
              Employs 550 with 250 exempt. Hires recent grads in accounting/finance,
              sales, engineering (mostly ChE and ME) and production/distribution
              management. Hires three co-op ChE's each year. Seeks experienced per-
              sonnel in accounting/finance, sales, manufacturing management,
              distribution, engineering, MIS, and laboratory assistants and chemists.
Procedure: Send resume to Manager of Employment,
              1310 Seaboard Industrial Blvd, Atlanta, GA 30318.
              (404) 351-1680

APPENDIX D: CROSS REFERENCES

If you have experience in a specific industry or are seeking a specific industry, these cross references should be most helpful and will steer you to the companies with the most active hiring in your field.

Advertising Agencies
BBDO/Atlanta
Ogilvy and Mather
Thompson, J. Walter
Tucker-Wayne/Luckie & Co

Airlines
See Transportation

Banks
See Financial Institutions

Black-owned Companies
Atlanta Life Insurance Co
M & M Products
Russell & Co.

Certified Public Acc'nts
Andersen, Arthur & Co.
Deloitte & Touche
Ernst & Young
Peat Marwick Main & Co.

Colleges and Universities
Emory University
Georgia Inst. of Technology
Georgia State University

Consultants
Byers Engineering Co.
Heery International
Kurt Salmon Associates
Law & Co.
Law Environmental
Lockwood Greene
Simons-Eastern

Corporate Hq. Services
BellSouth Enterprises
BellSouth Mgt. Ctr.
Coca-Cola Corp.
Coca-Cola Enterprises
Electrolux Co.
Fuqua Industries
Nordson -- Division Hq.
Siemens Energy & Auto.
Southern Bell Employment
Southern Company Services

Wilkinson Sword Co.

Data Processing Centers
SABRE Group
SunTrust Data Services
Wang Regional Support

Data Processing--Hardware
Bull HN
Digital Commo. Assoc.
Digital Equipment Corp.
Hayes Microcomputer Prod.
Hewlett-Packard
IBM
NCR
Wang

Data Proc.--S'ware & Svcs
American Software
First Financial Mgt.
HBO & Co
MSA
Microbilt Corp.
National Data Corp.
Sales Technologies

Distribution (see also Mfg)
NCR--Worldwide Parts
Penney's Catalogue Distrib.

Fast Foods
Arby's
Chick Fil-A
Kentucky Fried Chicken
PepsiCo Employment Plus
Pizza Hut
Wendy's

Financial Institutions
Bank South
C & S National Bank
Decatur Federal S&L
First American Bank
First Atlanta Bank
First Union Bank
Fulton Federal Bank
Georgia Federal Bank
Trust Co. Bank
SunTrust Banks

Government
See Appendix F

Hospitals & Medical Svcs
Emory
Glasrock Home Health
Grady Memorial
Kennestone

Hotels/Motels
Atlanta Hilton
Courtyard by Marriott
Days Inns of America

Insurance and Insur. Svcs.
Allstate
Atlanta Life
Blue Cross/Blue Shield
Cotton States
Crawford & Co
Equifax Services
Life of Georgia
United Family Life
Williams, A. L. Corp.

Leasing
GE Computer Svcs

Manufacturing
Arrow Shirts
Ciba Vision Care
Coca-Cola Bottling
Ford Motor Co.
Foote & Davies
General Motors
Georgia Marble Co.
Georgia Pacific
Harland, John H.
Kuppenheimer Men's Clothiers
Lithonia Lighting Co.
Lockheed Georgia Co.
M & M Products
Mobil Chemical Co.
Oxford Industries
Schlumberger
Siemens/Automation
Siemens/Circuit Protection
Snapper Power Equip.

Southwire Co.
Zep Manufacturing

Manufacturing--High Tech
A T & T
Chromatics
Digital Commo. Assocs.
Electromagnetic Sci.
GEC Avionics
Hayes Microcomputer
Loral Information Systems
NEC
Northern Telecom
Oki Telecom
Panasonic -- Data Terminals
Rockwell--Missile Systems
Scientific Atlanta

Media
Atlanta Journal-Constitution
Cable News Network
Turner Broadcasting System
Turner Network TV

Non-Profit Organizations
American Cancer Society
American Red Cross
Arthritis Foundation
Institute of Nuclear Power

Office Products
Lanier Worldwide
Xerox Products

Property Management
Equitable R/E Investments
Portman Companies
Russell & Co.

Public Relations
Cohn and Wolfe

Publishing
BellSouth Advertising

Quasi-government
Federal Reserve System
Federal Home Loan Bank

189

Research/Develop. & Labs
- Amoco Fabrics & Fibers
- Centers for Disease Control
- Ciba Vision Care
- Coca-Cola USA
- Emory University
- GA Tech Research Institute
- Kimberly-Clark Corp.
- Lanier Worldwide
- NCR Software Develop.
- Scientific Atlanta
- Zep Manufacturing

Retail
- Athlete's Foot
- Big B Drugs
- Big Star Supermarkets
- Eckerd Drugs
- Haverty's Furniture
- Home Depot
- K-Mart Corp.
- Kroger's Supermarkets
- Macy's Dept. Stores
- Penney, J. C. & Co.
- Racetrac Petroleum
- Rich's Dept. Stores
- Smith, W. H. USA
- Upton's Department Stores
- West Building Supplies

Savings & Loan Assoc.
(see Financial Institutions)

Service Companies
- A T & T
- Credit Bureau
- Dobbs International
- Equifax
- Norrell
- Rollins

Stockbrokers
- Robinson-Humphrey Co.

Telecommunications
- A T & T Co.
- BellSouth
- BellSouth Mobility
- Contel Communications
- Contel Customer Svc
- MCI
- Southern Bell
- Telecom*USA
- US Sprint--Nat'l Accts
- US Sprint--SE Division

Transportation
- Delta Airlines
- Eastern Airlines
- MARTA
- Transus

Utilities
- Atlanta Gas Light Co.
- Georgia Power Co.

ATLANTA HEADQUARTERED COMPANIES

- American Cancer Society
- American Software
- Arby's
- Arthritis Foundation
- Athlete's Foot
- Atlanta Gas Light Co.
- Atlanta Journal-Constitution
- Atlanta Life Insurance
- Bank South
- BellSouth
- Blue Cross/Blue Shield of Georgia
- Byers Engineering
- C&S National Bank
- Centers for Disease Control
- Chic-Fil-A
- Chromatics
- Coca-Cola Company
- Coca-Cola Enterprises
- Contel Corp.
- Cotton States Insurance
- Crawford & Co.
- Days Inns of America
- Decatur Federal S&L
- Delta Airlines
- Digital Communications Assoc.

Electrolux
Electromagnetic Sciences
Emory University/Hospital
Equifax
Equitable R/E Investments
First Atlanta Bank
First Financial Mgt Co.
Fuqua Industries
Fulton Federal Bank
Georgia Federal Bank
Georgia Marble
Georgia Pacific Corp.
Georgia Power Co.
Glasrock Home Health Care
HBO & Co.
Harland, John H. & Co.
Haverty's Furniture
Hayes Microcomputer Products
Heery International
Home Depot
Institute of Nuclear Power
Kuppenheimer Men's Clothiers
Kurt Salmon & Assoc.
Lanier Worldwide
Law & Co.
Law Environmental
Life of Georgia
Lithonia Lighting Co.
Loral Information Systems
M & M Products
MARTA
MSA
Microbilt
National Data Corp.
National Linen
National Service Indus.
Norrell Corp.
Oxford Industries
Portman Cos.
Racetrac Petroleum
Rich's Department Stores
Robinson Humphrey
Rollins, Inc.
Russell & Co.
SABRE Group
Sales Technologies
Schlumberger/Sangamo Elec.
Scientific Atlanta
Siemens Energy & Automation

Siemens/Atlanta Serv. Center
Siemens/Automation Div
Siemens/Circuit Protection Div
Simons-Eastern Consultants
Smith, WH USA
Snapper Power Tools
Southern Bell
Southern Company Services
Southwire
SunTrust Banks
Telecom*USA
Transus
Trust Company Bank
Tucker Wayne/Luckie & Co.
Turner Broadcasting System
United Family Life Insur.
Uptons Department Stores
West Building Products
Wilkinson Sword
Williams, AL Corp.
Zep Manufacturing Co.

APPENDIX E:

PROFESSIONAL AND TRADE ASSOCIATIONS

Do not underestimate the assistance available through these organizations. Most industries are represented by more than one association, and the following list is only a modicum of the total number of national organizations. If your representative association is not included here, call the national headquarters and ask for the local contacts. Even if your association does not offer job assistance, you can still network through them.

Remember that many of the officers and contacts are not paid, but have volunteered their time to help the association. Do not ask to have long-distance phone calls returned and avoid taking up too much of the volunteer's time.

Also, please let me know of other associations that I have not listed here and who offer job assistance, so that I can include them in future editions. I would also appreciate comments on how useful and successful they are for you.

Alphabetical list of associations and organizations included

Ad 2/Atlanta
Administrative Management Society
American Association of Occupational Health Nurses
American Institute of CPA's/Georgia Society of CPA's
American Marketing Association
American Production and Inventory Control Society
American Society for Quality Control
American Society for Training and Development
American Society of Association Executives
American Society of Heating, Refrigerating and Air Conditioning
    Engineers
American Society of Personnel Administrators
American Society of Women Accountants
American Women's Society of CPA's
Art Directors' Club of Atlanta
Association of Records Managers and Administrators
Atlanta Ad Club
Black Data Processing Association
Business/Professional Advertising Association
Georgia Bankers' Association
Georgia Society of Hospital Pharmacists
Georgia Society of Professional Engineers
Institute of Internal Auditors
International Association of Business communicators
National Association of Accountants
National Association of Bank Women
National Association of Black Accountants
National Association of Women in Construction
National Black MBA Association
National Association of Legal Secretaries (Atlanta Chapter)
National Society for Performance and Instruction
National Society of Fund Raising Executives
Planning Forum
Public Relations Society of America
Purchasing Management Association
Society for Marketing Professional Services
Technical Association of the Pulp and Paper Industry

Appendix E:

Professional and Trade Associations

Note: The following information is believed to be correct, except that the names of officers and contacts may have changed, as was stated in the earlier text. If the contact listed here is not able to assist you, call the national headquarters of your association and request the name of the current local president. In addition, I would greatly appreciate information on other associations not listed here and that offer job assistance for their membership. Send the information to
Career Publications
P O Box 52291, Atlanta, GA 30355.

AD 2/ATLANTA
Comprised of advertising professionals under age 30, including recent college grads. Meets at Colony Square Hotel third Tuesday of each month at 6:00 for cocktails, followed by program; $7 for non-members. Primary career assistance is to help first job changers. Publishes monthly newsletter, but does not include job listings or seekers. Currently they have a Career Network Director that handles job and applicant match-up. They also sponsor a two-day Career Seminar in April of each year, mostly for recent grads. No charge for members, but must be a member to participate ($65/yr). For more information on career services contact the Career Network Director. For membership, contact the Membership Director. Both can be reached at
P O Box 18829, Atlanta, GA 30326.
(404) 264-6223 This is their answering service. Leave your name, phone number and the person you wish to contact, and they will return your call.

ADMINISTRATIVE MANAGEMENT SOCIETY
Members are office managers and small business owners. Publishes monthly newsletter which includes job vacancies and job seekers at no charge. Good networking system, although there is no specific job coordinator. Meets second Tuesday for dinner and program. Contact Barbara Funnell, Director of New Members at
1805 Roswell Rd, #25-A, Marietta, GA 30062.
(404) 565-3971

AMERICAN ASSOCIATION OF OCCUPATIONAL HEALTH NURSES

Corporate headquarters in Atlanta. Publishes monthly newsletter that includes both job openings and job seekers, usually five of each. Maintains a file for interested employers, and applicants are coded to preserve anonymity; listing information must be received by the fifth of the month prior to publication. Cost is $100 for companies and non-members; free to members. Does not meet monthly; rather, has large, national meeting in April and smaller, leadership conference in September. Employment information board is available at both meetings. For information, contact Public Affairs Assistant at 50 Lenox Pointe NE, Atlanta, GA 30324.
(404) 262-1162

AMERICAN INSTITUTE OF CPA'S/GEORGIA SOCIETY OF CPA'S

Excellent source for CPA's and non-CPA's. Has seven chapters in the metro-Atlanta area, representing geographic areas, and each meets monthly; visitors are welcome. Georgia headquarters maintains a Job Bank file which includes job seekers (average 50+) and job openings (average 15+). Membership is not required, nor is certification--there are many openings for non-CPA's. The Job Bank is updated monthly, with jobs deleted after one month; resumes, after three months. Also has listings for internships and applicants seeking internships. No charges for any of these services. For information concerning the various chapters and their meeting times and places, as well as for Job Bank information, contact the Membership Services Coordinator at
3340 Peachtree Rd NE, Suite 2750, Atlanta, GA 30326-1026.
404) 231-8676
Also publishes monthly newsletter which contains a classified ad section on the back page. Companies and individuals may advertise there for a fee of $30 for 50 words. To place an ad or obtain a copy of the newsletter, contact the Communications Department or ask for Allison Green at the above address and phone number.

AMERICAN MARKETING ASSOCIATION

The Atlanta chapter is one of AMA's largest, with more than 1000 members. Members are from marketing-related backgrounds, mostly research, advertising, planning and analysis, with some sales reps also. Meets second Wednesday each month for lunch, with usually 150+ present. Also has group called "Young Professionals," which meets monthly for career enhancement seminars. Publishes monthly newsletter, *Marketing Messenger*, which includes a column for job openings and job seekers (*must* be AMA member). No longer maintains resume file, due to the large volume they formerly received. For membership information, contact the Chapter Administrator listed below; to be included in the employment column, called "Atlanta Market Place," send a 40-word synopsis, a check for $30 and your AMA membership number to Joan Grashof, Chapter Administrator,
1868 Trumbull Dr, Dunwoody, GA 30338.
(404) 392-9972

AMERICAN PRODUCTION AND INVENTORY CONTROL SOCIETY

Membership comprised of companies and individuals engaged in manufacturing management and inventory control. Publishes monthly newsletter listing job openings and job seekers, and maintains a file for prospective employers. No charge. Membership is preferred, but not required. Meets for dinner on the second Wednesday each month. Contact David Howell, Placement Coordinator, at
c/o American Software, 470 East Paces Ferry Rd NE, Atlanta, GA 30305.
(404) 261-4381

AMERICAN SOCIETY FOR QUALITY CONTROL

Membership comprised of quality control administrators, including governmental, manufacturing, administrative, etc. Meets monthly and non-members can attend; the date varies. Publishes monthly newsletter for members, and includes job listings and job seekers. Generally, however, all employment assistance goes through one person who handles both job listings and job seekers, and also maintains a resume file. Membership is preferred, but not required. Send resume and contact Dr. Charles Wimberly,
c/o Southern College of Technology, Industrial Engineering Dept.,
1112 Clay St, Marietta, GA 30060.
(404) 424-7378

AMERICAN SOCIETY FOR TRAINING AND DEVELOPMENT

An educational society of personnel trainers and performance managers, both corporate and consultants. Must be a member of the association to use their extensive "Position Referral" service. Does not list openings or applicants in monthly newsletter. All job openings are distributed at monthly meetings (first Wednesday), but the prospective employer's name is not released. For information regarding the Position Referral Committee, meetings and procedure for joining, call or write the ASTD office at
6472-E Church St, Douglasville, GA 30134.
(404) 920-1457

AMERICAN SOCIETY OF ASSOC. EXECUTIVES (GA affiliate)

Represents the paid employees of more than 300 professional associations in Georgia. Send resume to office. Keeps resume on file for 90 days for perusal by interested employers. Publishes monthly newsletter which lists job openings. For information, contact Sharon Hunt, Executive Director at
2786 N. Decatur Rd, Suite 200, Decatur, GA 30033.
(404) 299-3559

AMERICAN SOCIETY OF HEATING, REFRIGERATION AND AIR CONDITIONING ENGINEERS, INC.

Corporate headquartered in Atlanta, and publishes monthly magazine with classified section. Local group publishes monthly newsletter which lists both

job openings and synopses of job seekers, available free to members only. To receive the newsletter and to submit your synopsis, contact Greg Ferguson at The Austin Co., 48 Perimeter Center East, Atlanta, GA 30346.
(404) 394-2500
National office: 1791 Tullie Circle NE, Atlanta, GA 30329.
(404) 636-8400

AMERICAN SOCIETY OF PERSONNEL ADMINISTRATORS

The Atlanta chapter has nearly 1000 members and meets first Monday evening of each month; non-members can attend two meetings, after which membership is required. Has Resume Referral Service Coordinator, who maintains a resume file for interested employers, and who also publishes a list of job openings (average 20+ monthly) that is available only at the monthly meetings--it will not be mailed. (The monthly newsletter does not include employment information.) For membership information, contact Debbie Mills, VP of Membership, at
1925 Monroe Dr NE, Atlanta, GA 30324.
(404) 881-9800
To have your resume included in the Resume Referral Service, contact Harold Price at
c/o DCA, 1000 Alderman Dr, Alpharetta, GA 30205.
(404) 442-4000

AMERICAN SOCIETY OF WOMEN ACCOUNTANTS

Publishes monthly newsletter that includes job seekers and openings, but without individual or company names. Local membership is preferred, but not required, especially for individuals relocating to Atlanta. Their service is not available to personnel agencies. Meets at Lanier Plaza Conference Center on the second Tuesday of each month for supper, a speaker and then the business meeting; current cost is $15. Yearbook is published for members, that includes companies and job titles of their membership. Send resume and references to Margaret Corbin, Employment Committee Chairman at
964 Oak Springs Ct, Stone Mountain, GA 30083.
(404) 299-3281

ART DIRECTORS CLUB OF ATLANTA

Members are creative advertising types: graphic artists, photographers, copywriters, production, etc. Meets at Trio Restaurant for cocktails on the second Tuesday each month. Publishes quarterly newsletter, but does not include job information. Maintains resume file, and matches job openings with prospective applicants. Membership not required. Contact Nancy West, Executive Director, at P O Box 94047, Atlanta, GA 30377.
(404) 266-8192

ASSOC. OF RECORDS MANAGERS AND ADMINISTRATORS

Publishes monthly newsletter "Arma-gram," which lists job openings and occasionally applicants. A confidential file of job seekers is maintained, and applicants are notified before being referred to a company. Usually meets third Tuesday of each month for dinner and speaker, but may vary to accommodate exceptional speaker. No charge for service and membership is not required. For information, contact Ms. Sam Yarbrough, Career Placement Chairman at c/o Paul, Hastings, Janofsky & Walker, 133 Peachtree St NE, Suite 4200, Atlanta, GA 30303.
(404) 588-9900

ATLANTA AD CLUB

Membership comprised of companies and individuals in advertising and advertising-related businesses. Has monthly luncheon on third Monday. Publishes monthly newsletter, "Ad Lines," which includes both job listings and applicants. Only member companies can list job openings and individuals can list for $5. For information and job listing procedure, contact Hugh Lovewell at 3340 Peachtree Rd NE, Suite 775, Atlanta, GA 30326.
(404) 262-1080

BLACK DATA PROCESSING ASSOCIATION

Call or write for membership information and meeting dates. Members can send resume to be circulated, and request to be added to the mailing list for the monthly newsletter, which lists job openings. Contact Willie Odoms, President, at P O Box 50462, Atlanta, GA 30303.
(404) 885-8638

BUSINESS/PROFESSIONAL ADVERTISING ASSOCIATION

Members are advertising managers, directors of corporate communications and other executives from advertising agencies, corporate advertising and industry suppliers (sales), that are involved in business-to-business marketing (not consumer marketing). Meets monthly (except summers) on second Thursday, for dinner and program. Maintains Professional Assistance Network (PAN) to help members with job search. Publishes bi-monthly newsletter (may go monthly) which lists job openings and seekers. For inclusion and to obtain a copy, write or send resume to PAN Coordinator, Stephanie Walsh, c/o Williams Printing Co, 1240 Spring St NW, Atlanta, GA 30309.
(404) 875-6611

GEORGIA BANKERS ASSOCIATION

Represents all commercial banks in Georgia. Publishes bi-weekly bulletin which includes job openings and seekers. No charge and membership is not required. To receive the bulletin or to list yourself, contact David Williams, Director of Communications, at
50 Hurt Plaza, Suite 1050, Atlanta, GA 30303.
(404) 522-1501

GEORGIA SOCIETY OF HOSPITAL PHARMACISTS

Call Job Hot Line at (404) 985-2345 for current openings with contact data.

GEORGIA SOCIETY OF PROFESSIONAL ENGINEERS

Eighteen chapters in Georgia. Publishes bi-monthly newsletter that lists job openings and refers resumes on file to interested employers. Has monthly meetings and major semi-annual meetings. Must be member to attend meetings and receive newsletter, and prefers membership in order to retain resume. For more information, including meeting dates and places, call Jackie Kimberly, Director, at
1900 Emery St NW, 1 Park Place, Suite 225, Atlanta, GA 30318.
(404) 355-0177

INSTITUTE OF INTERNAL AUDITORS

Members are auditors and accountants in private and public organizations. Grants the CIA designation. Averages 100 at monthly meetings on second Monday, except summers and October (first Monday) at Lanier Plaza Conference Center at 5:00; visitors are welcome ($25, includes supper). Publishes monthly newsletter, but currently does not list job opportunities. Maintains resume file, and has successfully matched applicants and openings; no charge. Contact Merwin L. Chambers, President and informal job coordinator, at
c/o M.E.A.G., 1470 Riveredge Pkwy NW, Atlanta, GA 30328.
(404) 952-5445

INTERNATIONAL ASSOCIATION OF BUSINESS COMMUNICATORS

Members are professionals in all areas of communications and public relations, working for corporations, as consultants or as freelancers. Members and non-members can participate in resume file and informal placement service by sending six copies of your resume and a confidential note to the placement coordinator summarizing years and areas of experience, and minimum salary requirements. Resumes are kept on file for three months unless renewed or removed. Publishes monthly newsletter, "Communicators Classified," that lists both job openings and seekers. The service is free to local members and employers, and costs $5 for non-members. All communication from job seekers except renewals is to be in writing. Ad will run only once unless renewed. Deadline is the 15th of each month. Send 40-word ad (plus contact data) + fee (if applicable) and resumes to Karen Hill, c/o C&S National Bank, 35 Peachtree St NE, 7th Floor, Atlanta, GA 30303.
(404) 581-3165
For membership information, write IABC Vice-President for Membership at PO Box 467654, Atlanta, GA 30346.

NATIONAL ASSOCIATION OF ACCOUNTANTS

Two Atlanta chapters, roughly representing northside (600 members) and in-town (250 members) areas, and each has an Employment Director. Northside group maintains a job list, rather than wait for the monthly newsletter, and you can obtain one by contacting Troy Hammett at c/o Hyatt, Imler, Ott and Blount, 100 Ashford Center North, Suite 200, Atlanta, GA 30338.
(404) 394-8800
Employment Director also maintains resume file for employers' perusal. Northside group meets third Tuesday each month at 5:00 for dinner, and also on the last Thursday each month at 7:00 am for breakfast.

NATIONAL ASSOCIATION OF BANK WOMEN

No formal job assistance programs, but excellent networking system. Publishes quarterly newsletter, but seldom includes openings or job seekers. Meets monthly, usually on the second Wednesday. For more information and to get into their network, contact Kelly Moran, President, c/o C & S National Bank, 6737 Londonderry Way, Union City, GA 32091.
(404) 969-3792

NATIONAL ASSOCIATION OF BLACK ACCOUNTANTS

Has monthly and quarterly newsletter that lists openings and job seekers. Maintains "Job Bank" of resumes for interested employers. Meets third Wednesday each month, and printed agenda includes job openings. Currently no charge for members or non-members. For information or to list, contact Ms. Bobbie Thomas, Career Development Chairman, at
64A Perimeter Center East, Bin 213, Atlanta, GA 30346.
(404) 668-3056 - office; 875-1711 - home

NATIONAL ASSOCIATION OF WOMEN IN CONSTRUCTION

Membership comprised of women in construction-related positions and industries. Operates very successful Occupational Research and Referral Service, matching jobs and applicants. Also publishes monthly newsletter which includes job openings and applicants, and maintains applicant file for interested employers. Also offers information on EEO-related positions. National Headquarters has computerized Job Data Bank. Awards annual scholarship in Atlanta area. Meets first Tuesday each month at 6:30; membership not required. Important: when sending resume, indicate WIC on envelope. Contact Eileen Witt at P O Box 939, Smyrna, GA 30081.
(404) 432-0151

NATIONAL BLACK MBA ASSOCIATION (Atlanta Chapter)

Publishes monthly newsletter which includes job vacancies. Meets fourth Monday of each month. Has book of openings for perusal at these meetings and resumes are circulated to attendees. Non-members can attend two meetings at no charge, after which they are expected to join. For information, contact Ms. Patricia Williams, President, at P O Box 158, Atlanta, GA 30301.

(404) 321-7581

NATIONAL ASSOC. OF LEGAL SECRETARIES (Atlanta Chapter)

Meets second Monday evening for dinner and program. Has Employment Chairman, who announces current openings at meetings and will refer applicants to existing openings; has far more openings than applicants! For information, contact Evelyn Brundidge, Employment Chairman, at City of Atlanta, Legal Department, South Tower, 1 CNN Center, Suite 1100, Atlanta, GA 30303-2705.
(404) 658-1150

NATIONAL SOCIETY FOR PERFORMANCE AND INSTRUCTION

Members are professionals in performance and instructional technology, with emphasis on increasing employee's performance and productivity; more emphasis on program design and instructional technologies, and less on platform instruction. Meets third Tuesday of each month from 5:30 to 8:15, and much networking is done then; past Membership Chairman found her job this way! First meeting is free for non-members, and $14 thereafter; $10 for members. No formal assistance, but monthly newsletter occasionally includes company openings. Contact Membership Chairman, Kathy Deprey at (404) 870-2469, or write P O Box 53306, Atlanta, GA 30355.

NATIONAL SOCIETY OF FUND RAISING EXECUTIVES

Membership comprised of professionals in the non-profit fund raising industry. Meets for lunch on the third Monday of each month, and job seekers are introduced to the membership present. Publishes a bi-monthly newsletter which includes job openings, but not seekers. Maintains a resume file for prospective employers, and acts as liaison between companies and applicants, matching job openings and seekers. Usually is aware of 10-15 current job openings. No charges for the service, and membership is not required. Contact David Martin, Executive Director of the Georgia Council on Economic Education at
807 College of Business Administration, Georgia State University, Atlanta, GA 30303.
(404) 651-3280

PLANNING FORUM

Members are mostly corporate planners and consultants, involved in financial planning, strategic management and business development. No formal job assistance, but excellent networking. Meets monthly on third Monday, except during summer, and visitors are welcome. For membership information, contact Josh Taylor at 5 Piedmont Circle, Suite 510, Atlanta, GA 30305.
(404) 231-9287
For other information, call Bennie Farmer at (404) 391-8288

PUBLIC RELATIONS SOCIETY OF AMERICA

In addition to monthly newsletter, PRSA publishes two monthly employment letters: "People Pointers," for full-time PR professionals; and "Resources," for part-time and freelancers. Both employment letters include job listings and job seekers. "People Pointers" lists an average of ten openings and 25 job-seekers each month. Members of PRSA receive all three letters free and can list in either of the employment letters at no charge, plus a file of resumes is kept for interested employers. Non-members can list in either employment letter for $10 and their resume will be kept on file, but they will not receive the monthly letters. The procedure is as follows: compose and send a 35-word synopsis of yourself, your resume and $10 fee (if applicable) to Denise Grant at 5108 Victor Trail, Norcross, GA 30071.
(404) 449-6369
Important: Deadline for job listing is the fifteenth of the month preceding the monthly listing.

PURCHASING MANAGEMENT ASSOCIATION

Local affiliate of National Association of Purchasing Management (NAPM). Has more than 500 local members and meets second Thursday for dinner and speaker; membership is not required, but encouraged. Job help is informal, but very effective, and is handled by the local president. The national head-quarters also sponsors a for-profit placement company, whose profits go to NAPM's education programs, and this agency maintains a list by state of job vacancies. For local openings and information, contact Don Vesko, the local President, at 608 Tree Mt. Pkwy, Stone Mountain, GA 30083. (Include a stamped, self-addressed envelope if you want job openings.)
(404) 786-9051 if out-of-state; in Atlanta, call 593-6224.
For information from NAPM Services, contact Carol Jamison, P O Box 22165, Tempe, AZ 85282-2165.
(800) 888-6276 x3010

SOCIETY FOR MARKETING PROFESSIONAL SERVICES

Membership comprised of companies and individuals in architecture, engineering, planning and construction, and who are responsible for marketing their organization's services. Has Employment Opportunity Committee under Director of Development, that maintains file of job openings and applicants and acts as a "clearing house" for employers and applicants. Quarterly newsletter does not include job information. Meets for lunch on the fourth Monday each month. Must be member to utilize service. For membership information and employment assistance, contact Pete Pruitt, Director of Development, at
4330 Georgetown Square, Suite 500, Atlanta, GA 30338.
(404) 457-5923

TECHNICAL ASSOCIATION OF THE PULP AND PAPER INDUSTRY (TAPPI)

Corporate headquartered in Atlanta. Maintains a resume file for prospective employers. Publishes monthly magazine, *Tappi Journal,* which includes a classified ad section at the end, listing job vacancies. Occasionally, job seekers also include an ad, but there is a fee. Send your resume or call them at P O Box 105113, Atlanta, GA 30348.
(404) 446-1400

APPENDIX F: GOVERNMENT OFFICES

(1) U. S. (Federal) agencies

(2) State of Georgia

(3) Local counties and City of Atlanta

GOVERNMENT OFFICES

Federal:

Office of Personnel Management (OPM)
     75 Spring St SW, Suite 956, Atlanta, GA 30303-3309
     (404) 331-4315 for recorded message; 331-4531 for assistance

Largest federal agencies in Atlanta:
     Environmental Protection Agency
     345 Courtland St NE, Atlanta, GA 30365
     (404) 347-3486

     Dept of Health and Human Services (including Social Security)
     101 Marietta St NW, Suite 1601, Atlanta, GA 30303
     (404) 331-2205

     General Services Administration
     Note: Prefers to hire recent grads under the "outstanding scholar" authority,
     which requires graduation in the upper 10% of class or 3.5 GPA.
     75 Spring St SW, Room 388, Atlanta, GA 30303
     (404) 331-3186

     Department of the Treasury--Internal Revenue Service, Atlanta District Office
     275 Peachtree St NE, Room 528, Atlanta, GA 30343
     (404) 331-6008

     Department of Labor
     1371 Peachtree St NE, Room 136, Atlanta, GA 30367
     (404) 347-7692 Ask for "Chief of Employment Branch," currently Marilyn
     Vanne.

General Accounting Office
     101 Marietta Tower, Suite 2000, Atlanta, GA 30323
     (404) 331-6900

US Postal Service
     3900 Crown Rd, Atlanta, GA 30304
     (404) 765-7234

State of Georgia

State Merit System
     200 Piedmont Ave, Room 418, West Tower, Atlanta, GA 30334

(404) 656-2724 - Two minute information recording, plus directions to their office.

Department of Audits
> Financial Division: Hires mostly recent grads with accounting major or with 25 hours of accounting, probably 15 each year. Good GPA is important. Send resume to Director of Finance Division, 270 Washington St, Room 216, Atlanta, GA 30334.
> (404) 656-2180
>
> Performance Audits Division: Hires mostly MBA's and accounting grads, but also seeks a few economics and public administration grads; good GPA is important. Send resume to Director of Performance Audits, 270 Washington St, Room 602, Atlanta, GA 30334.
> (404) 656-2006

Local

Atlanta, City of
Profile: Government for City of Atlanta, employing 8000+ and expecting an increase. Hires both recent grads and experienced personnel in accounting/finance, administration and MIS.

Procedure: Send your resume with Social Security Number and cover letter requesting to be placed on their mailing list for a certain job classification (*e.g.*, accounting, administration, engineering, etc.) and they will notify you of openings for which you can apply. If you are in Atlanta, you can go to their office and review the "Specifications List," which includes all current openings. Mail information or go to Employment Services Division, 260 Central Ave, Atlanta, GA 30335.
(404) 658-6164 to check on job information and resume status; 658-6161 for professional-level Job Hot Line.

Clayton County
Profile: Smallest of the five major metro-Atlanta counties, with 1600 employees. Publishes a Job Announcement List of current needs, which can be reviewed at their offices; they will not mail copies. You can call their office and ask if there is a job vacancy for your specialty, and if so, they will mail you an application form. Both recent grads and experienced personnel are needed.

Procedure: Contact or visit their office at
121 South McDonough St, Room 104, Courthouse Annex, Jonesboro, GA 30236.
(404) 477-3239

Cobb County
Profile: Third largest metro-Atlanta county, and growing rapidly. Currently employs 4000 total. Annually hires approximately 50 recent grads and 25 experienced exempt, primarily in accounting/finance, engineering (CE

mostly) and MIS (Unisys, may change), plus social work and urban planning. Seeks experienced managers in accounting and engineering.

Procedure: Send resume to Employment Manager,
Cobb County Personnel Department, 10 E. Park Square, Marietta, GA 30090-9614.
(404) 429-3266

DeKalb County
Profile: Second largest metro-Atlanta county, employing 5000+. All applicants are hired through the county merit system.

Procedure: Write for application from DeKalb County Merit System, 120 West Trinity Place, Decatur, GA 30030.
(404) 371-2331 - Job Hot Line

Fulton County
Profile: Largest metro-Atlanta county, employing 9000+. Has many openings in all areas. Must go to their office to review current job listing, then apply for employment. Most exempt positions require a proficiency test, which is given twice weekly.

Procedure: Go to their Personnel Office at 165 Central Ave SW, Atlanta, GA.
(404) 572-2382

Gwinnett County
Profile: For several years, Gwinnett County has been the fastest growing county in the entire nation, and is now the fourth largest metro-Atlanta county. Employs 2500, and expects an increase in hiring, both for recent grads and experienced personnel, especially civil engineers, accountants and other disciplines.

Procedure: Send resume to Personnel Department,
75 Langley Dr, Lawrenceville, GA 30245.
(404) 955-6506 - Job Hot Line; 995-6500 - information

About the author . . .

STEPHEN E. HINES has been involved in personnel recruitment and placement in Atlanta since July, 1970. He is
the founder and owner of HINES RECRUITING ASSO-
CIATES, a professional-level personnel placement service,
established in 1975. For more information, call (404)
262-7131, or write P O Box 52291, Atlanta, GA 30355.

The author wishes to thank those friends whose editorial
and professional contributions have been an invaluable aid
in the production of this book:
>
>Dick France
>Raymond Lamb
>Jeffrey Smith
>Charlotte Taylor